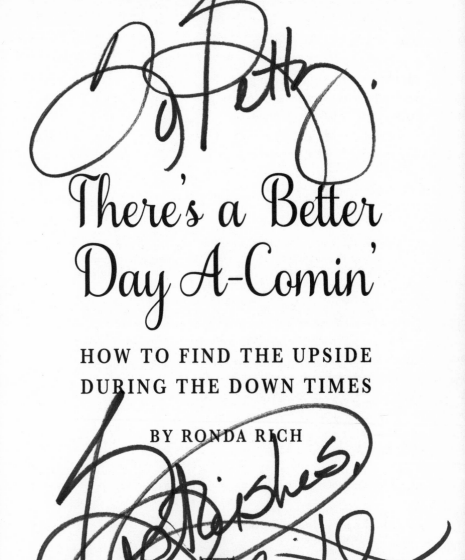

There's a Better Day A-Comin'

HOW TO FIND THE UPSIDE DURING THE DOWN TIMES

BY RONDA RICH

RUNNING PRESS
PHILADELPHIA · LONDON

Books published by Running Press are available at special discounts for bulk purchases in the United States by corporations, institutions, and other organizations. For more information, please contact the Special Markets Department at the Perseus Books Group, 2300 Chestnut Street, Suite 200, Philadelphia, PA 19103, or call (800) 810-4145, ext. 5000, or e-mail special.markets@ perseusbooks.com.

ISBN 978-0-7624-4725-1
Library of Congress Control Number: 2012942008

E-book ISBN 978-0-7624-4752-7

9   8   7   6   5   4   3   2   1
Digit on the right indicates the number of this printing

Cover design by Whitney Cookman
Interior design by Matthew Goodman
Edited by Jennifer Kasius
Typography: Baskerville and Samantha

Running Press Book Publishers
2300 Chestnut Street
Philadelphia, PA 19103-4371

Visit us on the web!
www.runningpress.com

Contents

FOR TINK
Who came along and brought
many better days with him

Friends Come and Go but Enemies Accumulate

I t is from the rural South that I rise up, a gift from great-great-grandparents who decided, whether on whim or intent, to follow rugged pig trails and primitive dirt roads down through the Appalachian mountains of the North to plant themselves and their future descendants in a place that would become storied for its challenges and sometimes bitter fights for survival.

To say it wasn't always easy for my ancestors would be a dramatic understatement—and I come from people who never understate. Starvation claimed some, disease claimed many, unpaid taxes claimed farms, and desperate times laid claim to each and every one. No one in my family escaped from the gnawing hunger of the Civil War years or from the sheer, heart-wrenching desperation of the Great Depression. But they hung on, believing in better times to come, if not for themselves then surely for their children and grandchildren.

"There's a better day a-comin'," one said to another so often that it became the mantra on both sides of my family, a promise stoutly believed and carried forth through ten generations of my people. For it is true—no matter how hard times get, they always, without fail, turn back to better times. Determined, sturdy people prevail. They always emerge as winners during losing times. I have only to look back at several generations of my family to know that.

Though the people who went before me were not formally educated—they were, after all, mountain people—they had strong intellects, a natural curiosity, and a sturdy propensity toward what they called "good common horse sense." Beginning with my great-grandfather William Bryson, ten generations back, who arrived in the Southern Appalachians in the early-1700s from County Antrim in Northern Ireland, my wily Scotch-Irish ancestors collected wisdom. It cost nothing to collect, but was more valuable than rubies or gold. They were mindful to look at the lessons of life and glean pieces of knowledge that would help to advise others in future times. They looked carefully for learning opportunities and studied hard on such things.

Then, owing to the Scotch-Irish gift for storytelling and belief in oral history, these pieces of wisdom were passed down, and each new generation was commissioned to carry forth with the instruction, "Whether you learn a lesson the hard way or, Lord willing, the easy way, share with others what you know." We were also taught to look for lessons in other people's lives, not just our own.

"You don't have to live it to learn it," Mama said. "You just have to be smart enough to see it, wherever it is."

From an early age, I have always been keen to grab hold of what others can teach me through both their successes and their mistakes. I am especially grateful to learn in a way that can enable me to miss potential sorrows. As a journalist, sports reporter, NASCAR publicist, writer, and speaker, my path has often crossed with legendary figures, as well as common folks with calloused hands, all who had a story to tell.

For example, there was Otis, the overall-wearing, big equipment operator who graded the land where I built a new house. Otis turned out to be a wealth of good advice. I listened intently to all he had to say, for his wisdom was solid and often downright funny.

"Main thing I know," he said one day as we shared a cup of coffee, "is that friends come and go, but enemies accumulate."

Now that is about the smartest piece of wisdom I've ever heard. Otis proved to me that you don't have to have a lot of book learning to be smart about life. You just have to have an open mind and be willing to receive life's knowledge from those who have learned it firsthand and are smart enough to process it and generous enough to share it.

"Now, you know," he began, thrusting his hands deep into the pockets of his overalls, "that you can't put no moonshine still on this river, don't 'cha?"

I bit my lip to keep my slight smile from breaking into a full fledged grin. "No, I didn't. Why?"

"'Cause this river runs east to west and you can only put a moonshine still on a river that runs north to south because it won't make. It'd be bad stuff." He paused and studied me for a moment. "Everybody knows that."

Though the great-grandchild of a moonshiner, I did not know that. I had just learned something.

Over the years, I've kept my eyes and ears open for the lessons that surround us. Sometimes they're found in a college football game, or in the lives of friends, or in the triumph of someone thought to be well past her prime.

On any given day, all the pieces and circumstances of life can fall into place and you can emerge as a big winner—even a surprise, come-from-behind winner. I was a part-time sports writer, still in college, when I was given the coveted assignment of covering the Cotton Bowl in Dallas, Texas, one of the NCAA's major bowl games. The number-two ranked, undefeated University of Texas Longhorns were matched up against the eighth ranked University of Georgia Bulldogs. It wasn't really a matchup. It was a scheduled slaughter with a 1 p.m. kickoff time.

The Longhorns were within grasp of a national championship. Their linebackers were twice the size of any guy on the Georgia team, and their running backs were leaner and quicker than the Bulldog runners. All the odds makers and even the most loyal Georgia fans were certain that it wasn't a matter of *if* the Bulldogs would be beaten but rather by how much they would lose. The Georgia Bulldogs were nothing more than scrappers, but scrappy dogs fight hard for any morsel of food they can get. They have to, if they are to stay alive.

It was a perfect, clear Dallas day on that New Year's when the two teams lined up in the legendary stadium. From the beginning, it was obvious that the Longhorns were off their game. Nothing went their way. Late in the first quarter, Georgia scored the first points of the game with a field goal. Texas was unable to score a touchdown but managed three field goals, which gave them a 9–3 lead with three minutes remaining in the game.

Astoundingly, a punt mistake by Texas allowed the Georgia quarterback to run seventeen yards for a touchdown. Georgia fans cheered with glee while the Texas fans cried out in despair. Astonishment swept through the press box. The Longhorns had been brought down on their own hallowed ground by a weaker, less experienced team. David had silenced Goliath. Georgia won the game 10–9 and the Cotton Bowl title and gold rings, and moved up in the final rankings. Texas suffered further disappointment when Miami upset number-one ranked Nebraska. Had Texas won, they would have claimed the prestigious national championship, but since the Longhorns had lost to the Bulldogs, the championship went to Miami. No doubt that loss still stings Texas Longhorns' players and fans.

With my own eyes, I had witnessed a remarkable event and learned a lesson that has stuck with me: Even when the odds are stacked against you, it is always possible to pull out an upset. Hope always abounds, even in the direst circumstances. The weakest can triumph over the strongest; the lesser can outdo the best; the smartest can be outsmarted.

A dear friend of mine and her husband are poultry farmers. When the economy sank, the poultry company for whom they were growing chickens filed for bankruptcy. My friends went from twenty chicken houses down to ten. It was an enormous financial blow. They held on by the skin of their knuckles for a couple of years, but finally there came the day when they had nothing left at all. The electric bill was overdue and there was no money to pay it. But if the power was turned off, the chickens would die in their unheated houses in a matter of hours. My friend walked the floor. She prayed. She fretted. She debated. Finally, she said to her husband, "I know this isn't honest, but we have no choice. Take a check to the electric company right before they close. That'll give us at least twenty-four hours to come up with a solution, but we can't let them turn off the power tonight."

She wrote out a check on an empty bank account. Her husband got into his truck and started for town but stopped at the mailbox first. In a matter of minutes, he came through the door, whooping and hollering. In his hand, he held a check for $100,000 that had come from a government surplus fund that had been set aside to help poultry farmers who had been impacted by the bankruptcy. That wasn't all. In the same batch of mail was a letter from their accountant with a refund check from the IRS for an overpayment from a few years previous. In a matter of minutes, their darkest day turned into celebration. They had gone from the depths of despair to utter joy.

There's always a solution to every problem and sometimes it isn't left to us to figure it out. Sometimes it's a simple matter of answering the phone, reading e-mail, or checking the mailbox. A better day often arrives when we least expect it, and sometimes it is bold enough to knock on our front door and throw itself into our arms.

In Los Angeles, I have a friend whose daughter, Jennifer, is an aspiring actress. Jennifer was sent by her agent to audition for a national Microsoft commercial. She was instructed to bring along her family because the casting director was looking for age-appropriate folks for family members. She took her mom and grandparents. Of course, her family only did it to help her out, because not one of them had any aspirations of being on television. Lo and behold, Jennifer's eighty-five-year-old grandmother was the one who was hired! At an age when few would expect her to work let alone act, she had landed an extraordinary part on a national commercial and ended up with a healthy paycheck that's making her golden years more comfortable. I fully believe that you could ask one hundred Hollywood producers and television executives if that was possible and every one of them would say, "Not a chance." But it happened.

It's never too late for a better day. Regardless of how challenging your life might be right now, you must hang firmly on to the belief that an upturn is coming. It always comes. Wherever you are in your life, there are many happy, fulfilling times still ahead. One may be waiting for you next month or in the early light of tomorrow morning. But it's coming, it's working its way toward you now. Every second of the clock takes you that much closer to a better day. No matter how the odds may be stacked against you, or how dark and desperate things are, or how old you are, anything is possible at any time. Meanwhile, revel in the sweet anticipation of that joyous time that lies just ahead because that's part of the fun. Plus, it helps carry you through the not-so-fun times.

I can't predict the exact hour or day of its arrival, but I have seen a lot of life and this I know: there's a better day a-comin'. Just wait and see.

CHAPTER 1:

Laughter Will Save You When Nothing Else Will

I f you live long enough, you will cross an invisible dividing line where you go from being the child of your parents to being the parent of your parent. And they will treat you just like you treated them when you were a teenager: they will defy, deny, dispute, and ignore you. You will, in short, pay for your raising just as your mama promised you would.

When that time comes, you will only survive it with laughter. Once I started addressing the exasperations and frustrations with comedy, my life changed. Before that awakening, I was constantly stressed, but when I started laughing, the world completely smoothed out. One morning I was in my office at home, working on a deadline for a project when my sister called. She was frantic. Daddy, who had just returned from a stay in the hospital, was sick again with a seriously upset stomach. Not only was he creating a mess everywhere, he was ill-tempered and staunchly refused to go back to the hospital.

"You've got to come over here and help me. Mama and I can't manage him, and he has to go back to the hospital."

I could have screamed. Once that emotion passed, I just wanted to sit down and cry. I had already lost so much time from work because of his stay in the hospital that I was way behind. There was no choice, though. I put aside my work and drove over to my parents' house.

My sister had not exaggerated. The moment I walked in the house, I could hear Daddy storming out loudly at Mama and Louise as they tried to help him and reason with him. When he saw me, he got madder. He knew that reinforcements had been called in to ensure that he went back to the hospital where he was bound and determined not to go. After about fifteen minutes of the yelling and carrying on, I knew something had to be done.

"Where's his nerve pills?" I asked Mama.

"In the kitchen, in the china cabinet," she replied. I turned on my heels and headed to the kitchen. Louise came running in, just as I was popping the top off the bottle and pouring the pills into my hand.

"Wait!" she exclaimed. "Don't give him one of those. I just gave him one. He can't have another pill so soon."

"It's not for him!" I yelled back. "It's for *me*!" She burst into laughter, then I started laughing, too. After a few minutes of laughing, our nerves were soothed and we were able to return to the business of getting Daddy to the hospital.

Daddy had already gained a reputation at the hospital for being cantankerous and difficult. Many men are like this particularly when they're elderly and having a hard time accepting the reality of old age. On his previous stay, he had pretty much pushed the nursing staff to its limit with his sustained grumpiness. The morning he was being released, a rather formidable nurse came in to give him medicine when he growled at her. She pulled back her shoulders, lifting her hefty bosom, put her hands on her plump hips, narrowed her eyes, and asked, "Do you know *why* you didn't *die*?" (He had come perilously close.)

He glared at her and, undaunted, she continued. "Because God didn't *want* you!"

I howled and even Daddy sniggered at that. He knew he was a handful.

One day I was taking him to the doctor for a checkup and from the time we pulled out of the driveway, he carried on terribly about my driving. "Turn here." "What are you doing?" "Don't get so close to that car!" I was a bundle of nerves by the time we arrived. In retrospect, it's amazing that I didn't wind up on nerve medicine for life. When the doctor came in to see Daddy, they were making small talk as he checked his blood pressure and I watched from a corner of the room.

The doctor smiled. "Well, you have perfect blood pressure."

"Of course, he does," I replied with a sarcastic snarl. "He doesn't *get* high blood pressure. He *gives* it!"

If you take life too seriously, it will break your spirit. When you lighten up and relax, you feel better and, importantly in times of crisis, you think clearer. Whether you're dealing with rebellious teenagers, an annoying spouse, or aging parents, your mental health will be salvaged if you can find humor in the situation. There is no medication that will calm you and carry you through a trying time like the gift of laughter. People sometimes feel that laughter is inappropriate during heartache and tribulations. And, truthfully, there are times when you can't joke around but, most of the time, you can find a way to laugh.

When Mama died suddenly of a brain aneurysm, I was stunned and devastated. She was laughing one moment in the foyer of my house, then lying at my feet the next moment. At the hospital, after the doctor had announced her death, my dear, longtime friend, Karen, was sitting with my sister, brother-in-law, Rodney, and me in the waiting room as we discussed the funeral. Karen is a very successful gospel singer. She has the voice of an angel, so I never hesitate to ask her to sing for people. It embarrasses her terribly. We were discussing songs for the funeral and had already asked Karen to sing. I suggested a song that was on a recent CD of hers.

"Sing it for them," I commanded and Karen, as usual, hesitated.

Rodney didn't miss a lick. "You treat her like she's your personal radio. You just turn her on and turn off whenever you like."

Now, we had just gone through the trauma of losing Mama and we were heavily laden with grief but it was so funny—and so true—that we cracked up. Immediately, the heaviness of sorrow lifted in the room. A while later, Karen and I were the last ones leaving the hospital. Suddenly, in the middle of the parking lot, I commented on Rodney's observation. We got so tickled that we stopped and laughed so hard that we were both holding our sides. Even in the dark shadow of death, there is nothing wrong with laughter. It truly is the best medicine, for it will soothe whatever ails the spirit.

At the funeral home, over a thousand people waited in line over two evenings to express their condolences. Friends and loved ones were especially aggrieved for us because it had been less than two months since we had stood in the same funeral home and mourned the sudden death of our brother. As is the case in tragedies and sadness, folks were eager to offer their help.

"If there's anything you need, just call me." And they mean it. At *that* moment. They do not mean it two weeks later because they've already moved on. I'm of the opinion that if you want something, ask for it *then*. Don't wait. I tried to think of what I needed. I had enough casseroles and cakes to last me a while, so I didn't need more food. I live on several acres and there is always a need for the pasture to be mowed with a big piece of farm equipment called a bush hog. That night whenever anyone asked me if I needed anything, I would reply straight-faced with a twinkle in my eye, "Do you bush hog?"

It stunned each person who asked but when they got the joke, we had a good laugh about it. It was a ridiculous request. Finally, my brother-in-law who was standing a few feet away and heard from the chuckling mourners about my request, came over, gripped my elbow tightly, and said, with a smile tugging at his mouth, "Stop asking everyone to bush hog for you."

I held my palms up and shrugged good-naturedly. "They all want to know if there's anything they can do for me."

"They don't mean bush hogging, dummy."

"But it's what I need. I don't need any more casseroles."

Of course, I was teasing but it certainly gave a lift to an otherwise darkly somber time. Not only did I feel lighter but so did the people who came through the receiving line. I gave them permission to be of good humor because I chose to laugh. Life is hard. There is nothing exceedingly smart about that piece of knowledge but here's something to consider: it's much harder when you can't find humor during the difficult times. Laughter is a salve for the prickles of life and salvation for a broken spirit.

A few months before Mama died, the local newspaper started charging for the obits. I feel fairly certain that this hastened her death because Mama was frugal, almost to the point of being stingy. She enjoyed the daily obituaries and read them word for word, whether she knew the deceased or not. Every time I stopped by her house when she was reading the paper, she started complaining and carrying on something awful.

"It's ridiculous," she fumed. "Do you know they charge by the word? It's gotten so expensive that no one can afford to put a decent obituary in there." The point here was that her daily entertainment had been shortened. She pointed that crooked little forefinger of hers and said, "Now, I'm telling you when I die, don't y'all put no big long obituary about me in the paper." I nodded. "I mean it." Her tone was getting firmer by the minute. I nodded again. She narrowed her eyes. "If you do, I'm not paying for it!"

I rolled my eyes. I knew she would be dead and it wouldn't matter how long the obituary was or how much it cost. "Okay," I replied.

"When I die," she continued, "You just put in the paper, '*I. Died.*'"

I said, "*O-kay.*"

When she died, Mama, who had become a folk hero of sorts through my newspaper column, was celebrated by many newspapers which announced her death in an official news story. One newspaper said simply, "Mama Dies." Readers knew who Mama was.

Now, Mama was always pretty proud of me but it's too bad that she didn't live to see what would have made her the proudest: I got her death in the newspaper for *free.*

CHAPTER 2:

It's Never Too Late for Things to Change

The world is full of teachers. Every person who crosses our paths offers an opportunity for us to learn. From some, we learn what to do, from others we learn what not to do. I once met a family of dreamers who were such doers that, against the world's wisdom of what was possible, they managed the impossible. Like many, I watched with astonishment as they tumbled out of the backwoods of Georgia and commanded the wide-eyed attention of the most brilliant engineers from Detroit to Germany.

Though they would go on to set speed records that still stand today, there was a time when the dream was literally seconds—yes, seconds—away from being over. Hope had tucked tail and run. There seemed to be no way to salvage the future as they had planned it.

George Elliott from Dawsonville, Georgia, was one of the smartest men I ever met. He was a mountaineer who combined "book learning," as his people liked to say, with an uncommon amount of common sense. He was clever, learned, and wise with the kind of mind that was constantly turning things over and over. Because he didn't look like an Oxford professor, people often underestimated him, a mistake that he was wily enough to use to his advantage. He was in his sixties when I met him, a tall, slender man with a head full of tousled gray hair, clear beautiful skin, and light blue eyes. More often than not, he was in work clothes—a short-sleeved button-up-the-front cotton shirt with his name embroidered over the left side pocket and navy chinos or the occasional pair of overalls. When he made up his mind to do something, he did it.

As a fairly young man, he, a lover of Coca-Colas, had been diagnosed with diabetes. "I walked out of that doctor's office and I never had another Coke," he told me once. "That was well over twenty years ago and I haven't had one since. I used to have one or two every day. I don't even miss them. I just made up my mind and I did it."

That's the thing about serious dreamers, the ones who always believe in a better day, they have a steely determination that allows them to put any setbacks or disappointments behind them. George Elliott never looked back. He never mourned over things that had gone differently than he wished. He picked up the pieces, analyzed them thoroughly, and extracted every bit of learning possible. Without question, Mr. George was one of my most important teachers in life. Just out of college when we met, I spent countless hours sitting at his knee or on the phone with him as he offered a tiny bit of what he had figured out about life.

"Quit" was a word that tasted bitter in his mouth. Though he and his dear wife, Mildred, lived simply in a tiny brick bungalow, he had scraped together a fortune, making himself into a millionaire from various business ventures, such as a lumber yard and a Ford dealership. A lover of cars and speed, he dreamed of building a NASCAR race team with his three red-headed sons: Ernie, Dan, and Bill. Like their father, all three boys possessed a strong work ethic and sharp minds. They had been taught early to work hard for an honest living and to stay focused on the family business.

George, who believed strongly in saving more than he earned, was a wise investor who looked for opportunities in everything from junk to real estate to gold coins. So, when he decided to put his family in the racing business in the mid-1970s, it wasn't a hobby. He was investing in the future of his sons and believed that with brilliant-minded Ernie building the engines, ingenious Dan assembling the transmissions, and talented, instinctive Bill driving the car, they could build a dynasty.

George and his boys, though, were the only ones who believed that. When the gangly, disheveled country boys showed up at the racetrack to take on the likes of Richard Petty, most people snickered among themselves. They paid no attention, though. What other people thought or said mattered little to the Elliott family. In fact, it mattered not at all. Like anyone who turns a dream into a reality, they were not dissuaded by the opinions of others. In fact, they didn't even listen. They put their heads down, focused on the job at hand, and stayed steady on the course. Oh, but what a sight they were, with a pit crew

made up of friends who were equally disheveled country boys.
To be underestimated is not a curse, it is a gift. Other
competitors made the mistake of shrugging off the Elliotts, so,
without scrutiny and the accompanying stress, they were free to
experiment and learn from what did not work.

For several years, the Elliotts plugged along, entering as
many races as possible while frugal George kept digging in his
pockets to fund the effort. After five years, George had
personally put a million of his hard-earned, diligently saved
dollars into the team, back in the days when a million dollars
was still the notable measurement of wealth. As much as he
hated to quit, as hard as it was to admit, it was time to consider
what he had always considered impossible: giving up.

"It nearly killed me," he admitted one day. "I believed in
what we were doin', but I couldn't put us in the poorhouse. No
amount of figurin' on my part could show me how we could
keep on. Finally, I had to tell the boys that I had spent every
penny I could."

It looked as though the end was inevitable and unavoidable,
so the decision was made to run the last race of the 1981 season
at what was then called the Atlanta International Raceway.
After the race was over, the Elliotts stood forlornly around the
Ford racecar.

"We couldn't stand loadin' up the car one last time,"
George explained. "We knew that once the car was in the trailer,
it was really over. We just kept standin' around, puttin' off
loadin' it up. We didn't want to go home because it was gonna
be a long, sad drive."

Dreams, though, often face what looks like certain death,
but if the dreamer is willing to push through, to keep trying and
believing, it is only a false death, a temporary loss of pulse. In

every situation, regardless of what it is, hope can disappear, but it is really only hiding around the corner, waiting for the right moment to resurrect itself.

Since the Elliott family had not been in any hurry to load up and leave, they were standing there as a short, stout, mustached man chomping on a cigar rounded the corner. He introduced himself as Harry Melling, a wealthy Michigan industrialist, who was looking to buy a race team.

"I've been watching you and I like what I see," he said, taking the cigar from his mouth and pushing his round cheeks into a smile. "I'd like to buy your team."

Quicker than a blink, George Elliott's dream bounced out of the intensive care unit and back to life and, oh what life there was. With Melling's money and their own incredible ingenuity, the band of ragamuffins transformed themselves into what they had always believed they were—winners. They defied the common belief of the NASCAR community that only teams based in the Carolinas could be successful because of the pool of talent available. With no one to help or mentor them, they did the best they could and the best for them turned out to be the best of the best. Their first year with Melling produced a pole position and several Top Ten finishes; the following year gave them their first victory, and then by 1985, they were setting the racing world on fire by producing cars and engines that could only be beaten when Bill got caught up in an accident of some kind. Once in Charlotte, several cars piled up in an accident but Bill deftly avoided it.

"I swear I'm not just sayin' this because he's my boy," George told me after the race. "But there's not another driver who could have gotten himself away from that mess."

They became the media darlings with their slow drawls and

quick ways, leading Bill to become the first NASCAR driver to grace the cover of *Sports Illustrated* after a record-setting year in which he won eleven races, eleven pole positions, and a million-dollar bonus, earning him the nickname Awesome Bill from Dawsonville. He and his brothers set speed records that will, in all likelihood, never be broken. Yet there was a time when it looked like the road had ended, that it was all over.

It's never too late for things to change, even when hope has retreated. Marriages that appear irretrievably broken can be repaired and made even stronger when least expected; a wayward child, who disappoints repeatedly, can transform into someone admirable; a job can appear suddenly where there have been no jobs; health can return and dismal finances can reverse. Better days take time to come, and sometimes we have to borrow all the time we can get, holding on until the last possible second. Don't let go too soon. Wrap your fingers tightly around the rope and hang on until your fingers have to be pried away from the rope.

The Elliotts were out of money and hope, but, stubbornly, they didn't go down easily or quickly. They bought every possible second, and by doing that, they went home that day overjoyed. They had awakened that morning certain that it was going to be a miserable day, but by the time the sun went down, their dream was full of life. What a life-changing, history-making difference a few hours made.

It's never too late for a situation to change or a better day to arrive. It's only too late when we give up and stop trying.

CHAPTER 3:

Mountains Are Moved One Shovel of Dirt at a Time

One morning when I went for a run, I looked over at a big pile of wood chips at the edge of my front yard. My uncle, in an extraordinarily generous effort, had brought a truckload of the chips and dumped them there. After several of his trees had fallen in a storm, he had them chipped up for landscaping use. Since wood chips are fairly expensive, and since I had a large gardening area that was in need of the coverage, he brought them to me. Soon, though, we discovered that it wasn't as simple as it seemed. The pile had some longer sticks in it that hadn't chipped up well, so when Brandon, who does my yard work, tried to shovel them up, it was very hard. Eventually, he gave up.

"Miss Ronda, that's just too hard to do," he said one day, appearing at my door with his hair wringing wet from sweat. "I don't know how you're going to move them."

Normally, Brandon is not a quitter, but he had found a mountain that had backed him down. I narrowed my eyes. "Oh Brandon, it cannot be that hard," I replied, a bit skeptical and a lot irritated. As soon as he left, I took a shovel and marched determinedly down to the pile only to quickly discover that Brandon was right—it was incredibly difficult. When I tried to push the shovel into the pile, the sticks that hadn't been chewed up completely stopped it. As a result, the shovel only picked up a few chips at a time. Soon, I was exhausted and had gotten nowhere.

The pile was about four feet high. I looked at it and shook my head and said aloud, "How will I ever get those moved, short of using a piece of heavy equipment like a backhoe?" I, too, gave up.

A year and a half passed and the mountain of chips sat there, untouched and unmoved. A few briar weeds were growing around the edge. It looked pretty rough. One morning as I ran by it during my jog, I thought, "If I don't start working on a way to move those, they will sit there forevermore in an unsightly mess." During my run, I made up my mind: I would work a little bit every day moving those chips and eventually I'd get that area in my yard back.

I started that morning. I plunged the shovel into the midst of the pile and, just like before, it was stopped by bigger sticks. This time, though, I was undeterred. Even if I was only moving a few chips at a time, I was still making progress. Time, diligent work, and perseverance would eventually win.

I stuck with it that morning for about an hour, during which time something interesting happened. After the first few meager shovelfuls, it got a bit easier. When I finished that morning, I had made hardly a dent, but I was encouraged. I was on my way to moving that mountain.

I returned the next morning. As I was moving one shovel toward the landscaped embankment, it occurred to me: This is how life's problematic mountains are moved, too. One shovel at a time. The mountains of life can intimidate us like the pile of wood chips intimidated Brandon and me. We might make a half-hearted attempt to work through them, and then give up and walk away, leaving the mountain there as a barrier between unhappiness and happiness.

Some of the problems we encounter in life can seem too big, too impossible to move, so we let them back us down. But if we roll up our sleeves, dig in, and stay on task, we can move any mountain of obstacles even if the work is excruciatingly slow. A mountain of debt is moved the same way, a few dollars at a time; weight is lost a few ounces at a time, and while it might seem small, even insignificant at the time, it leads to big results when added together. Just a little sacrifice can lead to big gains (or losses depending on what you're doing).

Daddy once found a mountain that he didn't want to move. He wanted to own it. It was one hundred acres of beautiful, rolling pastureland, and he dreamed of owning it for a cattle farm. It's almost laughable now to think that the land was considered expensive at one hundred dollars an acre, but it was the early 1960s when $10,000 was more than most households brought home, after taxes, in three years. A few years earlier, my parents had built a simple three-bedroom brick bungalow for less than $5,000. A major land purchase was out of reach.

Mama listened to Daddy and said, "Ralph, there's no way that we can afford that."

He continued to make his argument that it was a good investment and that he could raise cattle there for extra income to help pay for it, then sell it all in a few years. Mama trusted Daddy.

"Okay," she said finally. "We'll pinch pennies here and there and we'll make it work."

Mama was a good partner to have because she was an excellent money manager. She and Daddy both rolled up their sleeves and went to work. Every morning, she made homemade biscuits with sausage, bacon, and eggs, so she made extra and packed the breakfast leftovers for Daddy's lunch. Until that farm was paid for, Mama homemade every stitch of clothing that she, my sisters, or I wore. Only my brother and father had store-bought clothes and those were only what were absolutely necessary. Daddy, true to his word, began to raise registered Hereford cattle, buying and selling for a profit. Several years later, the farm was paid off, and Daddy sold it for many times what he had paid for it—even financing the purchase for the new owner and making a substantial amount of money in interest.

I was taught, "If it's worth having, it's worth working for." Each day, they made conscious choices to save money that would help to pay for something bigger and more financially rewarding than a new dress or a lunch at the diner.

It was the same with my mountain of wood chips: I made a conscious choice to work on it daily. It took three months of consistent effort, but eventually I won. The unsightly mountain disappeared, put to good use elsewhere. In the bargain, I had built nicely toned arms from the work. Which, by the way, is a side effect of moving those personal mountains—we build emotional muscle that will help us shovel away the next mountain that threatens to stop us.

CHAPTER 4:

Make the Choices You Can Live with _and_ That You Can Die With

Making a choice you can live with for the rest of your life is one thing but think about taking the choices you make to your deathbed. How would you feel if you were out of time and there was no way to recapture lost opportunities or to follow the dreams of your childhood?

There was a point in my thirties where life had crumbled into a shambles around me. I was newly divorced, downsized from an excellent job after a corporate merger and my father was dying. Anyone who has divorced knows it's all about starting over in every way possible, especially financially when income and savings accounts are split in half. Not only was I losing the sturdy guidepost of my life and my financial security, but with Daddy's illness, I was obligated by duty and love to stay and help care for him. Moving elsewhere for a job was simply out of the question. Everything seemed hopeless and I kept thinking that the best was behind me, that I was too far down the road of life to rebuild. As I was to learn, that is the way that society teaches us to think, not what is possible or realistic. My life was so deeply mired in unwanted change and apprehension that I did not know how to begin to find my way out. I was troubled at every turn.

One day, there came an emotional breaking point. Though we tend not to like these breaking points, they actually bring good news and a turn for the better. When we reach the end of a road and we collapse, it forces us to read the map again and find a new direction.

I was in my home office when the desperation of the situation hit me. I was overwhelmed, fear seizing my heart. I slumped against the wall, slid down to a puddle on the floor and began to cry. I was gripped by absolute fear to the point that I was finding it hard to gasp for air.

Somewhere in the midst of those tears, it occurred to me: I had before me the opportunity to do whatever I wanted to do. There was nothing to limit me because there was nothing left. If I chose the right attitude, I would have a new beginning, not an ending.

That's the wonderful thing about being at the bottom—you have gone down as far as possible. Anything else is up and onward. It's nice to come to that place where the falling stops.

As my tears dried and I sniffled pitifully, I thought, "What is it I have always wanted to do?" Then I asked the wisest question I have ever asked, "If I had only three months to live, what would I regret not having done with my life?" I don't know where that question came from, but it certainly was a game-changer, a life-enhancer for me.

Think about if a doctor told you that you had three months to live. Three months is not enough time to change the course you have chosen, but it is plenty of time to regret what you did not do. It would be nothing short of agonizing to ponder on dreams that you had cast aside or all the things you "meant to do" but never got around to them. There would be no complete peace in those final days.

I knew the answer. Since I was a little girl, I had dreamed of writing books. As a child of six, I would pack the family suitcase—a brown leather piece of Samsonite luggage which I still have—and go on a pretend trip to New York City on "book business." How a child in the rural South would even know that books were published in New York is beyond me, but our childhood dreams are truly a compass for our future.

Somehow I knew and it became the fantasy I continued to carry fervently in my heart for three decades. Yet I had done nothing to make that dream come true. Nothing. I had good intentions and would often say to myself, "One day when I write my book . . ."

I have come to realize this about our childhood pretend games: A child play acts what she was born to do. One friend, now a teacher, used to line up her stuffed animals and teach them. Another who became a successful entrepreneur played with a cash register, keeping a cash box from which she made change for family members when needed. Another, now a nurse, was always bandaging and taking the temperature of her dolls. A pastor friend preached funerals for deceased pets.

Too often in life, we get distracted, but finding it again is as simple as this: travel back to your childhood and recall your games. It is probably there, still hovering between the toys. Clear out the distractions and center your mind to find it. Listen to your inner self and not the voices of others who tell you what you should do with your life.

Right there on the floor of my office, I had a powerful epiphany. I knew that I had to do whatever it took to make that childhood dream come true. I had to give it my best try. If I failed, I could live with that and, importantly, I could die with that. But I could not die peacefully knowing that I had completely disregarded that dream, the one that had been there since I fell in love with books as a toddler.

That became my turning point. I began a journey toward becoming a published author, knowing that I would do everything within my power to make it happen. I did not know if I would succeed, but I did know I could approach my final days with absolute satisfaction in having given it my best efforts. I was on a mission to create peace for my final days.

Eighteen months later, an outline for my first book became the center of a four-day auction among several New York publishing powerhouses. That book became a best seller and continues as a successful book many years later.

On the day that my agent called when he read my outline and praised it as one of the best he had seen, I hung up the phone and screamed with joy. It was one of my happiest moments. A better day had come on the heels of complete devastation. My dream now was more than just hope. It was alive with reality and promises of more to come.

"Remember this day," a wise friend said. "Remember how happy you are right now because there will come a time when this becomes commonplace to you, so enjoy it now for all its worth." He was right. There were more books and more auctions to come, but that moment was electrifying and it meant more because I had come from a dark place of despair.

As long as there is breath in your body, it is never, never, never too late to get back on course and head toward the right destination. Do not let the dreams of your heart perish.

CHAPTER 5:

Be Prepared to Seize an Unexpected Opportunity

My friend Debbie and I were having lunch one day when the conversation turned, as it will with longtime friends, to folks who have graced our lives and in a couple of incidents, disgraced them. We began to talk about him, a guy we had known when we were young and totally optimistic about what the future would bring.

Very talented in his field of expertise with good looks and limitless charisma, he was destined to be a star. Or so it seemed. When a couple of opportunities bounced toward him, he missed the catch. He wasn't alert and on guard. As time went on, his bright future faded to gray and then he, too, faded away. Most have forgotten his name or the promise he held back then. I wonder if he has forgotten, too.

"Whatever happened to him?" Debbie asked. "Where is he now?"

I shrugged. "Who knows?" I paused for a moment, thinking before continuing. "The saddest thing is not those who are never blessed with opportunities but those who are yet they throw them away."

Nothing is more heart-breaking. Dreams, like opportunities, are fragile. We have to catch them gingerly, treasure them and handle them with care. Once they're dropped, few are ever picked up again. In order to find a better day, it's crucial to stay alert to opportunities that are easy to see as well as those that are hidden within a problem. Granted, sometimes it takes some "figuring" and "studying on" as my people like to say but if you look on it long enough and study hard enough, an opportunity as fine as gold will beckon.

This reminds me of a story I heard, about a woman who could have been caught up in the busyness and bustle of the airport yet she spotted an opportunity and boldly took advantage of it. That moment of courage would bring a lifetime of better days.

Glen Campbell is an entertainment legend. He is the singer of some of the best known standards in popular music and still remembered for the ground-breaking variety show, *The Glen Campbell Goodtime Hour.* He is also a sound businessman who wisely opened a music publishing company, which licenses songs to be recorded and performed.

By good fortune, I happened to be backstage several years ago at one of Campbell's concerts. In between the evening's two shows, I was sitting on a sofa when he dropped his long-legged frame down next to me and struck up a conversation.

"You're from Georgia, huh?" he asked. He glanced upward thoughtfully, a smile spreading slowly across his face. "Alan Jackson is from Georgia, too." He was referring to one of country music's superstars who, at that time, was the hottest singer in the nation. He shifted in his seat. "Let me tell you a story that happened to me in Georgia one time."

Campbell was caught between flights in the Atlanta airport. There he was flipping through a magazine while he waited for his next flight when a young, blonde flight attendant approached him.

"Mr. Campbell," he repeated, imitating a high-pitched female voice. "My husband is a singer and he writes songs. He's very good." She told the superstar entertainer about her husband, singing his praises. Courageously, she asked if she could send him a tape of some of his songs.

"I pulled out my billfold and gave her a card for the manager of my publishing company. I said, 'Sure. Just send it to this guy and tell him I told you to send it to him.'" He stopped at that point, tossed his head a bit and snickered. "I thought, 'Let him deal with it.'" He grinned. "I didn't want to be mean to her. She was a real sweet girl and she was just trying to help her husband."

The faithful young wife wasted no time in sending off the tape, following Campbell's instructions by saying something to the effect of, "Glen Campbell told me you would help." Of course by this point, Campbell had forgotten the encounter, but the manager, not wanting to bother his boss, didn't call to ask him. He just did as he was told. He listened to the tape and heard potential. That was how Alan Jackson, superstar-to-be, wound up in Nashville, writing songs for Campbell's publishing company.

Campbell began to sing a cappella—now there's a thrill—the lyrics to a song that Jackson had written for his publishing company called "Here in the Real World."

He stopped, shook his head. "That's a heckuva song." He laughed. "And it's made me a lot of money, too!"

"That's amazing," I commented. "Imagine the courage it took for her to come up to you. And think what would have happened if she hadn't."

He nodded. "The world might not have had one of the greatest songwriters and singers that Nashville has ever known. I'm pretty lucky, too. I was just trying to be nice, and it ended up making me a small fortune."

When an opportunity dropped down in front of her, Denise Jackson, a flight attendant, passing through a busy airport, saw it and embraced it. It's probably safe to say she wasn't expecting it, but when it appeared, she grabbed it. Because of her boldness, her husband became one of the most awarded singer/songwriters in the history of country music. Had she walked on by, the Jackson and Campbell families would have been much poorer indeed.

It's fitting to use Nashville's country music industry to point out an equally powerful missed opportunity. I don't know personally the guy who taught me this lesson, but his grievous mistake sticks strong in my heart as I know it surely must in his own. When singer competition shows became the trend, one cable channel launched a country music version. One season, the judges and audiences had narrowed the field down to eleven but the emcee announced that the television audience could vote to bring one back. An extremely talented guy was given a second chance. His talent, particularly as a songwriter, was riveting. An executive from the record company that was offering a contract to the winner was a tough, outspoken woman. She, however, was clearly enamored with the young man's talent, especially as a composer. Once after hearing a powerful composition of his, she said, "That is a career-making record. That's the kind that becomes a standard." The underdog became the big dog. He won and was signed to her label.

When I tried to obtain an interview with him for my syndicated column, his publicist turned me down. "He's not interested," she said a bit tersely. I could detect frustration in her voice.

I was stunned. "What? My column reaches a million readers weekly. He's not interested in that kind of publicity?"

"No. I'm sorry."

Later from another Nashville friend, I learned that the young man made it difficult for anyone to deal with him or help him.

"He's got an addiction," she said. "People who work with him are already tired of it. His career is going to be over before it gets started."

And it was. His record deal disappeared, and he hit rock bottom to the point that he went into rehab. A couple of years later, I was in attendance, along with many industry executives, of a showcase for a new group called Lady Antebellum.

As it happened, the record executive who had believed in the young man during the competition was there that night. We were introduced and began to chat. I found her to be extraordinarily lovely and sweet. After a few minutes, I had to ask about the young man. Her face clouded with sadness. She nodded, then sighed deeply. "It's the saddest thing. He could have been a superstar. He has talent, looks, and personality. He

had a once-in-a-lifetime chance. His addiction destroyed it."
She dropped her eyes for a moment, then said, "He wrote me a
letter and apologized. It broke my heart because he knows he
blew it. But what can you do? He had the kind of opportunity
that most people would die for and threw it away."

His is a lesson for us all. The saddest thing in life is not those
who have dreams and never have the opportunity to pursue
them but rather the ones with golden opportunities who
carelessly throw them away. Can you imagine living with that
regret every day of your life? Knowing that you had the dream
job, the perfect spouse, or the chance of a lifetime yet did not
protect it? I can imagine little else that would be as sorrowful.

There are two kinds of opportunities: those that are
embraced and those that are missed. Some we hold to our
hearts and others we drop through our hands. Every
opportunity, especially the ones that lead to big dreams, should
be treated like a precious gift: a one-of-a-kind, once-in-a-lifetime
gift. Because most of them are.

CHAPTER 6:

We All Have to Pull Together in Order to Pull Through

There never was an abundance of money when I was growing up. We didn't suffer from need, but as Mama often said, "You don't always get your wants. There's a big difference between needs and wants." That meant mostly that my clothes were homemade and every dollar earned was either slowly spent or wisely saved. We grew our own vegetables, and Mama spent most of the summer "putting up" jars of green beans, soup, and tomato while freezing corn, peas, and okra. We had chickens that provided fresh eggs and, for a long time, a cow that gave us sweet creamy milk, which could also be churned into buttermilk or butter.

Like most families, we had financial setbacks from time to time like a leaky roof or a water heater that just up and quit unexpectedly. There was one particularly hard time when an employee had stolen what to us was a small fortune from Daddy's car repair business. It put us in peril of losing both the business and our home, but Mama moved quickly to take a job in a sewing plant, working until all debts were paid. Throughout all of this, my parents diligently taught the necessity of helping others, even when we ourselves needed help. They had both grown up poor in the Appalachian foothills where those people, regardless of how little they had, always shared with each other.

"If you have a dollar and someone needs it more, give it to them," Daddy used to say. He adamantly believed that the more we give, the more we are blessed. "It is an honor and a privilege to be able to help someone in their time of need," he intoned with conviction. "It'll come back to you time after time because someone will always be there to help you in your time of need."

Daddy believed especially in giving, even when it was hard. "You can only help someone when they *need* helping. All the other times, you're helping, you're only pretending for the sake of your own conscience. Reach down deep and help when it isn't convenient or you hate to give up the money. That's when it counts the most."

I was well into adulthood before I really grasped what he was saying. It is a thoughtful gesture if you take a cup of coffee to a coworker because you stopped to pick one up for yourself but it is *helping* if the coworker is down with the flu and, despite the schedule strain, you make soup and deliver it or run an

errand for her. "Give till it hurts," Daddy used to say, "Then
you'll know you've done what you should."

One year as the days spun quickly toward Christmas,
Daddy proved that he was a man of his word even when it was
most difficult. It was a cold, gray winter's day and, as was the
daily routine, Daddy was playing host to a group of men who
wandered in and out of his garage during the day. They poured
cups of coffee into old, ceramic mugs, then settled down around
the wood burning stove. It is a ritual lost nowadays to our busy
world, but back then, you could always find several men who
stopped in the middle of their day to swap stories and
philosophies of life, religion, and politics at places like Daddy's
shop. No doubt a lot of wisdom was born out of those
gatherings.

That day, the subject of conversation was that real estate
taxes were due the next day. Daddy heaved a low sigh of relief
and explained that just that morning he had finished a repair
job that paid enough to give him exactly what he needed for his
taxes. Without looking down, he padded his pocket, took a sip
of coffee, and said, "The Lord is good. The money came in at
the last minute, but it got here just in time."

The words had barely left his mouth when the shop's front
door opened and a slender young man with blond hair falling
past his shoulders walked in, stepping across the cold concrete
floor with a hesitant, nervous gait. Shyly, he approached the
men who stopped talking and stared with unflinching gazes. He
cleared his throat and, in an uncertain voice, asked, "Is Ralph
Satterfield here?"

Daddy eyed him carefully. It was the early 1970s and boys
who looked like that with long hair and blue jeans were called
"hippies," and it seemed like, to him, that boys who looked like

that were usually up to no good. His steady gaze turned wary. "That's me," he said, without smiling.

He came closer, introduced himself, and gushed out his words in a nervous spray of quick syllables. "Someone told me that you might help me. I've been out of work and can't find anything. Do you need any help?"

Daddy shook his head, still a bit uncertain about the stranger. "This time of year is the slowest. I don't have enough work to keep any of us workin' steady. People don't spend money on their cars at Christmastime." He shrugged. "Not if they can help it."

The young man's crystal blue eyes clouded. He swallowed a lump of pride and nodded. "Okay. I understand. It's Christmastime and . . ." His voice trailed off and he dropped his eyes to the floor.

Daddy thought about the money in his pocket. Almost to the dollar, it was just enough to pay the taxes. Not even enough left for a hamburger and a Coke. He had been sweating it for the past two weeks, trying to put the money together. This year it seemed that coming up with the money had been harder than ever. Normally tenderhearted, Daddy thought about his own family and obligations, so he was firm when he said, "I'm sorry, son. My taxes are due tomorrow, and I have just enough to pay them. I'd help you, if I could."

He nodded. "I understand. Thank you anyway." He started to leave but turned back and said softly, "Me and my wife can get by without anything for Christmas, but if I just had a little for the kids. I hate to let them down."

He was halfway to the door when Daddy stood up from his chair. "Son, wait a minute," he called out while reaching in his pocket to get his billfold. He opened it and pulled out a bill.

"Would a hundred dollars help?"

Joy filled the young man's face, and he hurried back to take the money that Daddy offered. "Oh yes, sir! It'd help a lot. Thank you so much!" Daddy had just given away a sizeable amount of his tax money.

Over the years that ensued, both Daddy and the young man, Tony, would often tell the story, both filling in what happened for each after Tony left the shop that day. Tony, who had, indeed, walked on the wilder side, was uplifted by the hand of kindness he discovered in his time of need, a time when all hope seemed to have vanished. It was the beginning of him becoming an extraordinarily fine, upstanding man, one who would go forth to repeatedly touch other lives in need. "Man, I never forgot how someone who didn't even know me helped me and my family. He gave me money when he couldn't afford it himself," Tony said.

A skilled carpenter, Tony got back on his feet and made a practice of paying forward that kindness. Over the years, anonymous gifts have been sent to folks who never knew who the benefactor was or that it was begun by a man brave enough to give what he couldn't afford. Daddy had given until he felt the ouch in his heart and the emptiness in his pockets.

It was amazing, Daddy often said, what happened after the young man left, tightly clutching the hundred dollar bill. The telephone rang and it was someone calling about an urgent repair. By the time that Daddy locked up the garage that night, he had replaced that hundred bill with another and, in addition, added another one to go with it. He had been blessed to have the money he gave away, doubled. More importantly, he had given it to someone who would spend the rest of his days paying it forward to others.

In days of economic uncertainty, at times when the world can seem hopeless, we have to help each other even when we have little ourselves. Together, we can pull through until better times arrive. This is not a time to be selfish. It is a time to give with an open heart, even if it seems like you have little to give.

Once I was spearheading an effort to raise money for a young mother who had endured the insufferable loss of her six-year-old twins who drowned together. Holding hands, the girl and boy had jumped off a sandbar while playing at the lake and had fallen in deceptively deep water.

There wasn't money for one burial let alone two, so the community sent in donations and quickly a significant amount was raised. In the first mail that arrived was a hand addressed envelope. When I opened it, two crumbled one-dollar bills fell out. "I am a single mother, raising five children on my own," the note began. "I work two jobs but it is still hard to make ends meet. I can't imagine the pain of losing one of my children. This is all the money I have in my purse and, to be honest, I have no idea why I even have this much. But I wanted to give it."

All these years later, that handwritten note still sits on my desk to remind me that no gesture is too small when it comes from the heart. I take it out of the envelope from time to time and reread it.

Without question, that woman was blessed as much—if not more—as the people who sent in large checks. She didn't have much but she gave what she could and she gave it from deep in her heart.

No matter how tough times are for you, there's someone who's hurting even worse. If you find that person and share what you have—whether it's time, money, or labor—it'll uplift your spirits and theirs. Pulling together, we'll find that better tomorrow.

CHAPTER 7:

Sometimes You Have to Walk by Heart and Not by Sight

The glass front door opened with a *swoosh* that echoed within the nearly empty radio station, and a tall, slender young man with dark blond hair sweeping past his collar stepped into the reception area. He was dressed in jeans and a plaid shirt that buttoned up the front and wore dark sunglasses that covered his eyes completely.

The receptionist had left for the day and, as was the usual afternoon custom for me, I was sitting at a desk halfway down the long, wide hallway writing commercial ad copy. As a nineteen-year-old college student, the radio job was one of my three part-time jobs, the others being the newspaper and a dress shop.

"Hello!" I called cheerfully as the young man approached the reception desk and waited. He turned toward the sound of my voice. "May I help you? I'm the only one here."

He grinned and walked toward me. Something seemed off. The sound of a steady clicking against the light-colored tile floor caused me to drop my eyes downward from his face. A white cane. The good-looking guy was blind.

I introduced myself as he approached. "Hi there," he said, stretching his hand toward the direction of my voice. "I'm John Jarrard. I'm a songwriter." He lifted his chin proudly. "I grew up here, but I live in Nashville now. I brought by a tape of some of my songs. I thought y'all might listen and, maybe, play 'em."

It was the beginning of a sweet friendship, one that would bring me joy and endless inspiration. John Jarrard was one of the most extraordinary people who ever crossed my path. He was confident of his talent, committed to his dream, and relentlessly stubborn in pursuing it. Diabetes had robbed him of his eyesight after he graduated from college, and it became a vicious thief that would keep on taking for over twenty-five years. As expected, his blindness was a setback but certainly not a dream stopper. He set his jaw in the finest Scotch-Irish tradition of his people and carried on.

"John was remarkable," recalled a Nashville music executive who often watched from his window on Music Row as John persistently called on record and publishing companies, trying to catch a break in a business where breaks are few and far between. "I would look out my window and see him tapping along the sidewalk with his cane. Day after day, he'd be out there knocking on doors and pitching his songs. I admired him so much because I don't believe I could have been that brave. The rejection in this business is tough enough when a person is completely healthy."

"I lost my sight," he once said to me with a smile. "But I never lost heart. I knew what I wanted to do in life. I promised my parents that I'd get a college degree. I did and then I went after what I wanted more than anything—to be a songwriter."

When the gradual oncoming of blindness finally enveloped him in darkness, John was down but he wasn't out. With his usual determination, he set about learning to maneuver on his own, acquiring skill and a sixth sense. I was taking him home one night in Nashville after a concert we had attended and, flawlessly, he directed me to his house.

"We should be passing Avery on the right," he said and I looked over to see that we were directly in front of the street sign. "Two more streets down is Hickory." A minute later, he continued. "This is Hickory." Sure enough, we were right there. It was like a magic trick.

"That is unbelievable!" I exclaimed as he continued to issue precise directions even as we talked and I lost track of where we were going. That was typical John, though. He never lost track of his journey, either emotionally or physically. He always stayed the course, determined to reach his destination.

Born the son of a cotton mill worker in a small rural town, John never suffered from limited vision. He believed what we all should believe—that every person has the same chance of finding his dream as the next person. Regardless of how grand it is or how remote it seems. The dividing line between those who succeed and those who fall short is perseverance, an attribute that can be any person's—just for the trying. You don't have to inherit it or be gifted with it from birth. Perseverance is yours for the choosing. How wonderful is that? It is your choice to either give up or push through the hard times. *Your choice.* You can quit or reach down deep inside and pull out that reserve of perseverance that lies within the spirit of each person.

Few things ever came easy to him. Adversity, though, soon found it had met its match, for John Jarrard, time and time again, spit into the eye of the devil and kept marching toward a future he could so clearly see with his heart. It took a few years and repeated discouragement, but John got a break because that's what happens if you keep wading through rejection— something good will eventually happen. And it did: He landed a staff writing position with the publishing company owned by the wildly successful country band, Alabama. Within a few years, he became one of Nashville's most colorful, most beloved, and most successful songwriters, composing his way toward twelve number one records.

One evening after John had earned a place of respect and success, we were at a celebrity stock car race at the Nashville Fairgrounds. John was a huge racing fan and loved attending races because he could hear the action and feel the vibration of the cars. A record executive came over to speak to us.

"I just heard George's (Strait) finished cut of 'Clear Blue Skies,'" he said. "Awesome!"

John, the song's cowriter, grinned from ear to ear. "Aw, man, that's great!" A George Strait album cut is sweet money to any songwriter but a Strait single is manna from the heavens because it rains royalty money.

"It'll be a single," the executive continued as John shivered with excitement. By then, success was commonplace for him, but he never lost a childlike enthusiasm. "It's a hit." And so it was, becoming yet another number one song for the man who refused to give up.

The last time I saw John, he was wheelchair bound after the amputation of both legs and a finger and his kidneys were failing. A deep weariness shadowed his face, the likes of which I had not glimpsed before, but his spirit, as always, was stubbornly resilient. I bent down, took his hand and whispered my name.

"I'm so glad to see you," I said. "I just love that new Tracy Lawrence record," referring to his latest number one song. "It may be my favorite song that you ever wrote. Don't you just love the twin fiddles on that arrangement?"

He threw back his head and laughed heartily. "You say that about every one of my songs—that it's your favorite."

I laughed in return. "It's so hard to choose." I squeezed his hand. "I'm proud of you. I'm always pulling for you."

He nodded. "I've always known that."

When the news came that John was in a Nashville hospital fighting for his life with his body rejecting a second kidney transplant and a threatening lung infection, I was concerned but not worried. I had long grown accustomed to him winning whatever battle he faced. This time, though, victory escaped him. At forty-seven, he had written his last words, leaving behind pieces of a remarkably strong heart scattered between the lines of his songs.

A warrior of courage and resilience, he is remembered as much for the fight as for the triumphs. Whenever my own ambitions falter in downcast circumstances, I recall John's struggles and the recollection infuses my dreams with renewed energy. The possibility of success, screams his legacy, can only be erased if we ourselves apply the eraser.

John lost his sight literally, but often we can lose it

figuratively if we don't guard against it. The future becomes dark and murky, our view obscured. It seems hopeless and not worth the energy to daydream of a brighter day, a time when those dreams can become a reality. As John proved, it doesn't have to be that way. Though diabetes stole much from him, John refused to let it wrestle from his grasp the greatest vision that a person can possess—that of seeing clearly a dream and marching sure-footedly toward it. He was blind to the world as others could see it but not blind to what others could not see— his dreams. Though he lost his eyesight, he never lost his heart. He dug in with tenacity, overcame serious physical disabilities, and triumphed. Oh, how he triumphed.

Dreams can hide from our line of vision. They can slip behind a problem or mistake and become invisible. But it is up to us to choose whether the loss of sight is permanent or temporary. I suppose when John lost his sight in his twenties that he was tempted to think that the best part of his life was over. But, in truth, the next twenty plus years were his happiest and most successful. His cherished dream became a reality. Despite a horrendous setback, his best days were still coming.

May his legacy stand forever and remind us all that sometimes you have to walk the path to a dream by heart and not by sight because sight can fail you but a determined heart never will.

CHAPTER 8:

You Have to Forget in Order to Completely Forgive

Without question, the most popular character who has ever appeared in my weekly newspaper column was my mother. Readers often howled at her antics and motherly haranguing, for they all understood and identified with those stories. After all, everyone has a mother.

Mama, for her part, was normally a good sport when I told a story where her tart-tongued diatribes or clever one-liners had put me in my place. I knew enough to always let her win, to allow her the upper hand because there is a certain respect owed to motherhood. I didn't want to alienate readers by Mama-bashing. When she joined me at speaking events, always sitting in the front row, she laughed the hardest at the story I often told of a book signing I did in Oxford, Mississippi. The event, held in a warehouse-like space, included a reception with wine and cheese. Now, Mama was a Southern Baptist teetotaler. It is safe to assume that I was smart enough not to be drinking wine in front of my mother.

I was standing toward the back of the room, talking to a woman who, while holding a glass of wine in her hand, was trying to find something in her purse.

"Here!" she exclaimed, thrusting the glass toward me. "Hold this for me."

No sooner was that glass of wine in my hand than Mama saw it and came charging with great purpose across the room.

"*Ronda Rich*," she said in that menacing tone that mothers use. "Is that a *glass of wine* in your hand?"

I looked down at the glass of Chablis, registering a look of shock. I raised my eyes and gasped in a mock tone of despair. "Oh my gosh, Mama, it was *water* when I picked it up."

But once I wrote a column that did not set well with her. She had had a triple bypass. The first couple of weeks of her recovery, she was angelic. There could be no better patient than she was. As time passed, though, her mood changed tremendously. She was hard to manage, grumbled about everything, and became downright hateful as she said the meanest things. By the time I took her back for her six-week checkup, my nerves were shot and I was at risk of losing my own pleasing personality. In front of her, I told the doctor how ornery she was.

"*You* need to give *her* something for her hatefulness because she's driving *me* crazy." I punctuated the command with an authoritative nod and crossed my arms across my chest.

Mama, hands folded in her lap, sat with an angelic smile, the picture of sweetness. The doctor studied her chart quietly, then looked at me and shook his head. "Nope, I'm not giving her anything. This is typical behavior of someone who has been on the bypass machine. It'll pass with time, and she'll return to herself." He smiled sympathetically. "But I'm not giving her anything for it."

My mouth dropped. "You can't give her anything for it?"

When he shook his head again, I pointed at him and said, "Then *you* need to give *me* something for *her* hatefulness because she's driving me crazy!"

When I wrote this story for my column, adding more details concerning her orneriness, it made a new person out of her: a new meaner, madder, more upset person. Oh my. I just thought she was bad before but it got much worse when the story appeared in print. I had finally gone too far. I bribed her for forgiveness with new clothes and trips. Eventually she forgave, albeit begrudgingly. She was much slower to forget and found her chance for revenge when readers began to urge her to tell stories about me that might be equally unflattering.

I agreed. At least to a certain extent. "Listen, you write my column for me one week. We'll call it 'Mama has her say.'" She was delighted and began to work on it. Of course, I vetoed many of the stories she suggested, but she plotted on nonetheless. She was filled with absolute glee over the prospect.

"You just wait, little girl," she'd said with a mischievous glint in her eye. I would twist uncomfortably in my seat because I knew that truth be told, Mama had much harsher stories to tell on me than I could ever find on her. She worked on it off and on for a few months, refusing to share her information.

"You're not going to tell the prom story, are you?" I furrowed my brow.

"Maybe."

I bit my lip. "Rory Hester?"

She snapped her fingers. "I forgot about that!" She grabbed her notepad and began to scribble. I tried not to show it, but I was unnerved.

When she died unexpectedly a few weeks later, I found the notebook with what she had written, still unfinished. It read, "I have people tell me all the time that I should write about Ronda like she does me and tell some bad things about her. But there are no bad things. I've forgotten them all. I only remember the good."

Tears filled my eyes as I realized that true forgiveness comes when we completely forget all about what or who hurt or angered us. People will sometimes say, "I'll forgive but I'll never forget." It can't be done. As long as you remember even the least bit of hurt, there is not full forgiveness and until full forgiveness comes, the best of better days cannot come. Sure, you'll have better days for they always come along, but the *best* of those days come when your heart is free of resentment, bitterness, and regret. You have to take those emotions and release them to the wind, let them blow away from you forever.

An acquaintance who had a grand dream and tried to pursue it, but could never make it happen has spent twenty years looking back. "I can't help it," he said one night, his pale blue eyes drilling mine. "I'm so bitter. I know I was better than some of those clowns who made it, but I didn't get the break. It eats me up."

Yes, it does. He can't forget what he sees as an injustice and he can't forgive it, so it has imprisoned him and held him back all these years. Had he freed himself, there is no doubt that he could have achieved much more than he has.

Later when a friend hurt me repeatedly over the course of several months, I replayed every hurt, every word, and every injustice repeatedly in my mind. Anger kept building. I was owed an apology. Several, in fact. And, of course, I fueled my hurtful anger by rehashing it with girlfriends who, dear friends that they are, sympathized and emphatically agreed that I had been treated terribly.

Every morning when I jogged, I thought of all that had occurred. I magnanimously assured the good Lord and my friends that as soon as he came to his senses and apologized, I was going to be extraordinarily gracious and accept. Then one day as I was running, I had a strong sense in my spirit that I had to forgive before I received an apology and let the forgiveness stand regardless. I thought of Mama and her words and realized that the path to forgiveness begins with complete forgetfulness, hard to do for someone who has an excellent memory like I do.

Surprisingly, it only took a couple of days to get to that point. Every time that my mind wanted to bring to the front anything that had happened, I pushed the thoughts away. I stopped having conversations with myself or anyone else about the injustices. As soon as I retreated from dwelling amidst the memories and forgot the details, I was able to give full forgiveness. I felt like a new person in heart and spirit once I had tossed away the heaviness of that hurtful grudge. Today, we have an extraordinary relationship, and I realize that if I hadn't taken the high road, I would have missed out on such happiness. If someone has hurt you, stop dwelling on it.

My sister called me one day to ask about the details of a

spiteful occasion when someone had lied about me, causing deep hurt. She had run into the person and faintly recalled what had happened years before. I tried to oblige. But I was unable to bring to mind any details. I recalled one or two broad pieces but nothing else. My sister, of all people, knows my excellent memory. I knew she was baffled, so I said, "You know what? I have put that out of my mind because it was so painful that I can't remember much about it."

Mothers love their children unconditionally, therefore, they don't harbor grudges or disappointments. They forget, forgive, and move on. It serves as a good model of behavior for all of us. It may sound like a cliché to say it hurts us more than it does the other person to hold a grudge, but it's true. Most people—you and me included—never even realize what hurt or damage has been caused. Some hurts are unintentional. If we hold on to them, we are inflicting conscious pain on ourselves, not the offender.

After all, do you ever think about any person you might have hurt in some way? What about the people that you might have hurt and never had a clue? Does it gnaw at you daily, sitting like a stone in your heart? Do you grimace every time you think of the person whose feelings you hurt?

See? I rest my case. Drop the unnecessary baggage and free yourself up so you can embrace the best of the better days. If you ever wonder how to do it, just remember your mama and forgive others the way she forgave you.

CHAPTER 9:

Dreams Are the Compass for Finding Your Right Direction in Life

Jeff Foxworthy is a courageous dreamer who is bold of spirit and brave of heart. He has gone toe-to-toe with the risks required by his dreams, looked those challenges in the eye, and stared them down. As in any combat, he was sometimes a bit wounded, but he always picked himself up and kept going back to fight another day.

Jeff has a calling, a dream which embedded itself in his heart with great passion. He is funny and talented; he is a terrific writer; and, most importantly, he connects with an audience. He sees life from a common man's point of view, one that he can dress up with humor. He unites people who see either themselves in his comedy or someone they know. He is also extremely blessed to have a wife who is a partner in every sense of the word. Gregg Foxworthy is beautiful inside and out with an incredible instinct and almost innocent-like savvy that has been instrumental in guiding her husband and his phenomenal career.

With what many would call a "safe" job at IBM, Jeff was appearing in local Atlanta comedy clubs as a hobby. From the beginning of their relationship, Gregg set her mind that whatever her husband wanted, she would help him to get it. Not many wives would think it was a keen idea for her husband to quit a $32,000 job with full benefits in 1984 and take up starving on the comedy circuit, but Gregg did. She believed fully in Jeff's talent and innately knew that he had the potential to make it as a comic.

It wasn't easy for a long time. Big, out-of-the-box dreams are hardly ever easy. Most come with a requirement of sacrifice, devotion, and lots of hard work.

"The first year we made $8,300," Jeff recalled with a slight laugh. "The next we made something like $14,000 and we really thought that was something."

That income was made with Jeff working fifty weeks a year, Tuesday through Sunday. Gradually, he would inch his way up in revenue, but he worked his way into near exhaustion by playing five hundred shows a year for eight straight years.

"We moved up real fast and was soon playing regular dates at the top comedy clubs," he said. "I had one goal from the beginning—to be on Johnny Carson. To our generation, that was it. Everyone told me that it would take ten years of working the comedy circuit to do it." Jeff's one of the most humble guys in the world, but he is a goal-setter and takes self-satisfaction in achieving those goals. He set his mind to appearing on Carson's *Tonight Show*. He started sending tapes to the show but, time after time, year after year, the tapes were returned, unopened.

"We lived in Smyrna, Georgia, and they weren't interested in anyone who lived outside of Los Angeles," he explained.

Meanwhile, he kept working steadily and, as often happens with those who work diligently on a dream, a creative piece of good fortune fell in his lap when he was inspired to write a bit of comedy about "You might be a redneck, if . . ." It started out as just a segment of his routine, but it quickly gained hold. His first book of redneck comedy was published in 1987, after being turned down by fourteen publishers. A small press in Atlanta showed interest in the project so the publisher asked Jeff, "How does $1,500 sound?"

"I kinda froze and didn't say anything," he remembered. "I didn't know if he was asking me to pay or not and I didn't have $1,500."

The publisher was offering an advance of $1,500 which, it would turn out, would be an excellent investment. That first book went on to sell four and a half million copies. After less than four years of scraping to get by and paying his dues, Jeff Foxworthy was on his way.

But he still couldn't get on Carson's show. And, until he did that, he couldn't hit the legitimate big time of comedy. Gregg had a solution. She had been acting in the Atlanta area but had been working to get a comedy club franchise. She had everything arranged and ready to launch when she decided to put her plans on hold for the sake of her husband's ambitions.

"I knew we had to be in Los Angeles in order for him to get on Carson," she said. "They only booked comedians who were living there. He was out on the road working so I called him up and said, 'I'm going to Los Angeles. I want to pursue my acting career.'"

Foxworthy was stunned. "Are you going without me?"

Of course she wasn't. Her entire plan was to get him to take the plunge and move to L.A., something that he had long resisted. "I knew that he wouldn't go for himself but he would go for me." The clever ploy worked and the happily married couple began their adventure and what an adventure it became. They emptied their savings account to buy a new Jeep Cherokee, then proceeded to load it down with two cats and everything they owned in the world.

"The night before we were packing because we were going to leave early the next morning," Jeff said. "My dad and his wife came over and had a knock-down, drag-out fight. They wouldn't leave. They just kept fighting and we kept packing. They finally left and we got to bed about 1 a.m."

The dawn that greeted them, brought with it a rare, pea-soup-thick fog which prevented them from leaving until noon. Two and a half hours away—the cats screaming the entire time—they stopped for gas in Birmingham. As they waited at a red light, another car came careening toward them, sideswiped them on the driver's side and drove off. They waited for the police to arrive who said, "There's nothing we can do."

An incredible rain storm had shadowed them, so they decided to stop for the night. It had been a hard day. "We stayed in seedy motels because that's all we could afford so every time we stopped, I had to carry the TVs into the room so they wouldn't get stolen," Jeff explained. "We had bought a big bag to put on top of the car which was guaranteed not to leak. Completely waterproof. When I took the bag in and we opened it, it was a baby swimming pool. You couldn't have put it in the ocean and had more water in it."

It was then that the Foxworthys, in despair, sat down and took a look around the low-rent hotel. The past twenty-four hours had been a disaster. "I think I might have had tears in my eyes," Jeff confessed. "But I said to Gregg, 'We've made a mistake. We shouldn't have done this.'"

Dreams, though, are a powerful compass. They will direct us through the dark of night when the way seems long and we think we are lost. Worldly wisdom will nudge us to think we're going the wrong way, that we're making a mistake. Finding a long-held dream can be scary because the bigger the dream, the bigger the risks, and the bigger the chances that obstacles will pop up. The Foxworthys faced that moment of fear and doubt, but they swallowed it down, stood together, and journeyed on. As they now recall, there was nothing about the one-week trip that was pleasant or relatively easy. Still, they pushed on. Though they knew no one in L.A., Jeff had met a friend on the comedy circuit who let them live in his apartment.

A couple of weeks after their arrival in Hollywood, Jeff performed at the Improv. In the audience that night was the talent coordinator for the *Tonight Show*. He followed Jeff out and asked, "Why haven't we had you on the show?"

Jeff laughed. "Because you keep sending back my tapes." A week later, Jeff Foxworthy reached his singular goal of appearing on Carson's show. It had taken him five years and two months to get there.

In those days, Carson signaled his absolute seal of approval for a new comic by inviting him over to the desk to chat.

Otherwise, he either clapped or gave a thumbs-up.

"I had six minutes and six minutes only. I had practiced and practiced to get my timing right but I didn't account for the audience's applause. Suddenly, I had to start editing out stories, which wasn't easy because I did them in sets. I had to think ahead of myself and edit out the weakest jokes. Somehow I did it and ended right on time but I was literally the most exhausted I've ever been." Because Jeff had worked hard to hone his craft and, by that point, had appeared onstage almost three thousand times, he was ready for his big moment. He had the experience to make it work under challenging circumstances.

"I finished and I was scared to look over at Carson. Finally, I did and he waved me over." It was a triumph. Immediately after that *Tonight Show* appearance, his career moved to the big time. Club audiences banded together to vote him the American Comedy Award and Showtime offered him a special. He was well on his way to becoming an iconic performer.

"Life sometimes comes down to holding your nose and jumping in," he said with the perspective of looking back. "I wouldn't have gone without her pushing me." He smiled at his pretty wife. "She believed in me more than I did."

"Do you ever think about what if you had given up that night in the motel room and turned around for home," I asked.

He nodded quietly. "I would never have known."

And look what he would have missed.

If you have a strong pulling toward a vocation, education, or mission, listen to the voice of that compass. It's a live GPS guiding you to where you are meant to be in life. Yes, there will be challenges but if you stay the course, there will be rewards, too. Nothing could be sadder than coming to the end of your life and not knowing what would have happened if only you had tried.

CHAPTER 10:

Never Give Your First Instinct a Second Thought

olly Parton is incredible. She is a whirlwind of energy who is constantly working and is never stale creatively and who uses her fame and fortune to help many. The Dolly Parton Imagination Library was her gift back to her native Smoky Mountains to promote literacy by gifting age-appropriate books to children each month from birth to first grade. It is now used by towns and communities across the nation.

Like countless others, I was a recipient of her generosity and kindness when she read a book I had written. She sent a lovely note on her signature butterfly notepaper (she loves butterflies) and even wrote an endorsement for the cover of the book. Whenever possible, she never turns away from giving a helping hand. There's only one Dolly, as her friends and colleagues often say, and that's really too bad. She is a remarkably talented woman who is a brilliant businessperson. Her brand is uniquely her own, and it didn't happen just by chance. She shrewdly plotted and strategized every step of the way, starting way back in the 1960s when she graduated from high school and struck out for Nashville. She, knowing that her looks promote a certain image, has always laughed off the dumb blonde jokes.

"I know I'm not dumb," she quipped with a cheerful wink. "And I know I'm not blonde!"

It's not just her smarts that has made her into one of the world's most famous women. She owes a great deal of credit to her instincts and she, unlike many of us, is unerringly faithful to that guidance. Everyone who knows or has ever worked with Dolly Parton will quickly attest to her intuitive nature and how, over the course of her career, she has always followed her first impulse, never second-guessing it. Even when a hunch was counterintuitive to the traditional wisdom of the entertainment business or when those closest to her strongly warned her not to take a professional risk, she always stood by her instinct. In the late 1970s, she rode it to international superstardom when, against the advice of others, she left Nashville to try her hand in Los Angeles. The result was hit pop-tinged records, movie roles, television shows, and a Broadway score, making an East Tennessee mountain girl into a one-name icon. Mention "Dolly" and everyone knows who you're talking about.

A few years before she took on Los Angeles, she had trusted her instinct on something that was again counterintuitive. Dolly Parton is one of the most prolific songwriters that any genre of music has ever produced. She has written over three thousand songs, among them numerous hits, while, incredibly, she has never cowritten a song. Most songwriters will, at one time or another, align with others to write songs. Not Dolly. She says that the creative process works best for her when she works alone.

One day when she was feeling a bit melancholy over a professional split with her musical mentor, Porter Wagoner, she had poured her feelings into a haunting good-bye song. She recorded the song herself and had a modest hit with it. Then, she was astounded to receive a call that Elvis Presley wanted to record it.

In an interview with CMT, she explained that she was thrilled. "Colonel Parker, Elvis's manager, called me and said that if Elvis recorded it, I had to give him half publishing on the song," she said.

That is a significant percentage to give away to someone who had no participation in writing the song. Of course, Elvis recording the song was a sure ticket to a platinum smash, which would have certainly loaded her bank account down with dollars and taken her to a new level as both a songwriter and moneymaker. It was a standard offer that Parker, a legendary shrewd businessman, often made to songwriters.

She wasn't even torn in her decision. She was sad, but she knew what she had to do—she thanked them kindly but turned them down. Again, others shook their heads in disbelief, but she forged ahead, believing in her instinct.

"I've always looked at my songs as my children. I expect them to support me when I get old," she explained with that trademark high-pitched laugh.

That business savvy served her well. She later recorded that song as a duet with country superstar Vince Gill and had a major hit with it, but it was Whitney Houston's version of "I Will Always Love You" on the soundtrack of *The Bodyguard* that, to date, has sold over twelve million records, earning Dolly millions in royalties. And not one penny did she have to split with anyone else. She knows what we all should never forget— our first instinct is an incredible compass along the path of decision-making.

If our instinct says it, we should just do it and never question it. If we all followed this rule, if we all followed our gut every time it kicked in, we'd reduce our mistakes and our stress substantially.

Yet, we don't.

Society teaches us that cold hard facts should prevail over instinct and common sense. In an information-driven age, instinct is getting pushed out more than ever. Our greatest successes come when we instinctively choose our course of action, particularly when it flies in the face of reason or other advice. Often times it is very hard to go against those we trust and who we know want the best for us. Yet it is a mistake to trust someone's well-meaning advice and disregard that little internal voice. Your instinct is uniquely yours, custom-designed to guide you along a journey that will work best for you.

I once met a guy at a dinner party who came over and introduced himself, telling me that he had wanted to meet me for a while. He sat next to me at dinner and was charming. However, I saw something in his eyes that felt like a warning, screaming "stay away!" I was inclined to do just that, but four of my friends knew him—they said they knew him "well"—and that he would be perfect for me. They pushed me to go out with him. At first, I clung to my instinct and refused but eventually I reasoned that my friends had to be right. After all, they had all known him for a long time so who was I to judge from one meeting? I dated him, and it turned out to be a terrible experience. Had I listened to my first instinct and not the well meaning encouragement of my friends, I would have missed out on a good bit of upset. Who needs more stress these days?

The next time your intuition strongly directs you down one path, don't hesitate, don't stop. Just keep going where it leads, and you will like where it takes you. If, though, you give in to peer pressure or analytical reasoning over a strong nudging instinct, you most surely will regret it.

CHAPTER 11:

A Prayer Answered Quickly Is a Faith Builder for a Prayer Answered Slowly

My great aunt Fairy was one of the finest women to ever draw a breath. Named Caroline at birth, her tiny size and ethereal-like beauty caused someone to exclaim admiringly, "She's so pretty. She looks like a little fairy." The nickname stuck but she did not live a fairy-tale existence. She was a hard-working woman who did backbreaking work, laboring beside her husband, Oscar Cannon, on their farm in the mountains. It seemed unfair that someone as sweet and pretty as she, with her light eyes, blonde hair, and gorgeous pale skin, should have such calloused hands. Over the years, she developed a slight stoop to her shoulders from the heavy load that she always carried in both body and spirit.

Theirs was a pretty farm with a crystal clear creek that ran down by the side of the barn and twisted through the front yard. Aunt Fairy and Uncle Oscar believed steadfastly in the power of prayer, depending on God to see them through the hard, uncertain years of the Depression. They had eight children of their own that they were trying to keep fed, but when my daddy, a thirteen-year-old boy, had run away from home, they took him in and finished raising him. They simply stretched the food a little further, eating less themselves if necessary. As an adult, Daddy was always quick to point out that he learned from Aunt Fairy the power of prayer in small things as well as big ones.

Rightly so. She had prayed her family through surviving when many of their neighbors were starving and losing their farms to taxes. After she and Uncle Oscar died, he well into his nineties, that farm sold for a handsome amount, a sum she surely could never have imagined during the days of one-dollar-an-acre land. Her old black Bible, well worn, promised her that God was faithful to supply the needs of those who prayed and trusted. Time after time, she took him up on that promise, using prayer to call forth rain on crops that were drying up, children suffering with maladies, or even for an old, run-down milk cow that needed to hang on for a while longer. In those prayers and others, God proved himself faithful to his Biblical promise, and in the bargain, these answered prayers buoyed her faith and prepared her for the real test to come, a time when the voice of the Lord seemed to have fallen silent.

Having survived the Depression by the skin of their overworked knuckles, Aunt Fairy and Uncle Oscar watched as those they had lovingly raised in their small white clapboard farmhouse, including Daddy and their son, J.C., took off to fight foreign wars. Daddy headed to the South Pacific while the Army Airborne sent J.C. to Europe. And, of course, she prayed over them for a safe return. Every night, she humbled herself to her knees on the old wood plank floor and faithfully petitioned God to bring the boys home safely. J.C., who had been drafted in February, 1942, was among the first troops to arrive in Italy. Fifteen months later, he was among a crew of six in a B-26 shot down over the Mediterranean. His parents were notified that he was missing in action.

Fairy and her sister-in-law, Bessie, would often walk a couple of miles to church and pray for his return. She believed it was possible. After all, God had answered her smaller prayers over the years, so there was reason to believe her biggest prayer to date could be answered. A year went by, the army notified his parents that he had been declared legally dead and that a funeral was in order. As any mother would, she sat down and cried. Uncle Oscar, always a pragmatist, began preparations for a funeral at the little white clapboard country church, Mount Pisgah, just a short ways up the road from their house. Dressed in their best clothes, the country folk gathered to sing mournfully, pray somberly, and remember sweetly the tall, handsome, smart boy who had died in service to his country.

A couple of hymns had been sung when Aunt Fairy abruptly stood up and stopped the funeral because she had a strong feeling that he was alive. "God promised me that He would bring my boy home and I believe He will." She turned on her heels and walked out of the church.

There was no funeral that day. God, of course, had not spoken in an audible voice to Aunt Fairy, but He had spoken into her spirit and given her peace of mind, an understanding that if she walked on faith—a faith that had been tried and proven—and not on sight or earthly wisdom, she would see a just reward.

A year later, the war ended, and on one of the first U.S. ships to return from Europe was her boy. The one God had promised her that He would bring home safely. For two days after being shot down, they had drifted in two raft boats, fighting off sharks and starvation until they had been spotted by an Italian enemy plane and captured. Except for a three-month period when he had escaped before being recaptured by the Germans, he had spent much of the war as a prisoner. The train delivered him to Atlanta and a bus took him to Gainesville. A ride with a mail carrier, then with a school bus driver got him back to the family farm. Still unaware that her beloved son was alive, Aunt Fairy was doing her morning milking of the cow when he appeared, mere skin hanging onto bones, in the barn.

"She threw her milk bucket into the air and jumped up to hug me," he remembered.

Without a doubt, it was one of the happiest moments of her life, if not THE happiest. Aunt Fairy, undergirded by all those smaller prayers that God had answered over the bare, starving years, trusted him with the biggest prayer of her life. For three years, she waited and believed, and in the end, her faith delivered.

Though she was a modest woman about her faith and

refused to discuss it too much for fear of bragging, she once told Daddy while they talked at her kitchen table, "I just held to the hand of the Almighty God," she said. "I knowed He'd not let me down. I had done seen too much to know any different."

Imagine three years of believing against facts, against the official declaration of the army that her son was dead, of being the only person who believed. It's astounding, really. Though troubled and tried on every side, she resolutely stood her ground, not just for a season, but for years. When all was said and done, Aunt Fairy, a robust-spirited mountain woman, was right. And the world's most superior government was wrong.

In a foreshadowing of what was to come, J.C. had dreamed before his enlistment that his mother received a package of his belongings—a straight razor edged in amber, a billfold embossed with wings, and a white silk scarf. Though he did not own any of the items at the time of the dream, those were exactly the things she received after she was informed of his death.

Stand your ground. Don't give an inch to naysayers or those who would have you discouraged. Miracles happen all the time. Why shouldn't you receive a miracle when you most need one? If you will practice your faith over the smaller things in life, then you'll be ready to fight strongly and assuredly when the big tests come your way.

CHAPTER 12:

Don't Let a Setback Keep You from Winning Again

I t was always fascinating to me as a kid why mistletoe grew in bunches high in towering oak trees. When winter came and the oak trees were bare of leaves, we could see thick bunches of it stuck throughout the trees, mostly in the tops of the oaks. If Mama wanted to decorate with it for Christmas, Daddy would trudge through the pasture, toting a shotgun, until he found the prettiest bunch. Then, he'd raise the gun to his shoulder, aim, and shoot it out of the tree.

I couldn't figure out how the mistletoe got there. Why on

earth did it grow so high up in the trees?

"The birds spread it," Mama explained one day when I was twelve. "They eat the berries, then fly off to another tree and leave the sticky seeds through their droppings or from the sticky residue on their beaks."

Seeds of wisdom, I have discovered, are sometimes spread throughout our lives by folks who are just flying through and stop for a momentary break. We may never see them again, but the wisdom they drop lingers forever.

Such was the case with Indy 500 champion Tom Sneva, who, most likely, will never remember the evening he sat by me in a press box at a local short track race. No doubt he never thought of me again after he left, but I have never forgotten our conversation, and importantly, what he taught me that night.

I was a college senior and had never heard of Sneva when the handsome man was introduced to me. Someone whispered that he had won the Indy 500 a couple of years earlier and, in those days, nothing was more prestigious than an Indy 500 win. He pulled up a chair, and we began to talk.

One of the most valuable gifts you can give yourself is an interest in other people and their stories. The art of asking questions will draw people out, encourage them to share their experiences, and give you wisdom that will help you down the road. Wisdom travels to us down three roads: our own experiences, the experiences of others who teach us, and the accumulation of education through reading, searching, and absorbing knowledge.

Some people learn little from anything, including their own experiences. That's sad but it happens. A key area where many people fall short in obtaining wisdom is failing to look at the successes and failures of others and learning from them. Every life is a teacher, and every person is a student. We only have to sit up and pay attention.

I asked a lot of questions that night as I often do. Sneva, to his credit, wasn't offended that I knew nothing about him. He seemed to find it refreshing and opened up to me with honesty. He had had a steady job as a high school teacher, sometimes filling in as a school bus driver, when he had decided to pack up his wife and children and move from Spokane, Washington, to Indianapolis and pursue his love for speed in 1973. A couple of years later during the Indy 500, Sneva had suffered what is still considered one of the most stunning, dramatic crashes in Indy car history when he had touched wheels with another driver, had flipped into the catch fence, and the car had torn in half, flames engulfing it. To all who had viewed it on national television, it had been terrifying. Imagine how it must have felt being in that car. The driver is securely strapped into the car, so it's difficult to escape, especially quickly. But Sneva did, though he suffered severe degree burns.

"How awful!" I exclaimed then propped my elbow on the arm of the chair, dropped my chin into my cupped hand, and leaned closer to hear more. His description of the accident had been mesmerizing. "Did you ever think about quitting after that?"

He shook his head. "No. Quitting never crossed my mind." He folded his arms, tilted his head, and continued, "But I did wonder if I would have what it took to win again. Even in the hospital, I knew I would go back to racing but what I didn't know was if I would have what it took to cross that line to be a winner." The school teacher in him, perhaps, caused him to pause a moment, gather his thoughts, then continue, "There is a line that every successful racer has to cross to win, that little bit of extra that pushes you to the edge and makes you a winner. I didn't know if I could cross that line." He shrugged. "That's what I didn't know."

That's understandable because an accident or a bad experience can push us into a place of wanting to be safe, a place where we take fewer risks. Especially for a man who has a wife and children. His doubt was surely increased because his brother, Edsol, had been critically injured in an open-wheel car accident several months earlier and was, at the time, in a coma. He died ten months later. I suppose in times like that a man thinks of his parents, especially his mother, and considers what losing another child would do to her. Any man with a decent heart loves his mama and doesn't want to hurt her in any way. That must have weighed on Sneva as he recovered, along with thoughts of his wife and daughters. I suppose Sneva considered how foolish his dream might seem to others when he could go back to the safety of teaching school and building a pension instead of risking life and limb.

A better day comes, though, when we meet a wall of adversity and, instead of retreating to safety, we push through. The very best days lie on the other side of impossible. The faint of heart and weak of spirit never know the best that life has to offer because they allow themselves to be stopped cold by a setback.

Sneva was neither faint of heart nor weak of spirit. And luckily, his injuries didn't leave him permanently disabled or disfigured. He climbed back into the racecar, pushed the doubts and fear away, and became the first driver to qualify for the Indy 500 with a speed of 200 mph. Talk about a comeback. He not only was able to cross that line, he crossed it in record-setting speed and won the national championship that year, the first of two consecutive titles. For several years, he could do no better than a second-place finish in the coveted Indy 500 but, finally, in 1983, the crowd cheered as he took the checkered flag. Tom Sneva had refused to back down from what could have been a crippling setback and, as a result, he saw the very best days of his life and career.

Two of my friends suffered similar setbacks from broken marriages to men who turned out to be untrustworthy, devious, and unfaithful. One's husband, as it turned out, was the complete opposite of who she thought he was. When he lost his job, he didn't tell her and pretended to go to work every day while borrowing from friends and family in order to deposit a "paycheck" weekly. He also had been married before but had never told her. Of course, she was stunned into devastation when the truth emerged.

The other friend's husband lived such a dishonest life that he lied even when the truth worked better. She refused to believe her friends, stood up for him, and, in essence, made something of a fool of herself because they were right.

The two women, though, handled their situations completely differently. The first one, cover-girl beautiful, chose to shut down completely and never trust a man again. As the years passed, she acquired a hard, mean look to her once soft, pretty face. She scowled when men asked her out, and when she did go, she found a laundry list of things wrong with them. She became cynical and bitter. Twenty years later, she is still alone and maintains that's what she prefers, that she will never trust a man emotionally and intimately. It's sad to say, but her best days are behind her because she was unwilling to push through a major setback and find a better day.

The other friend gathered her courage and said, "I can't let this get the best of me. I can't let it keep me from finding love again. I'll be more cautious, but I won't give up." Wisely, she took time to heal before she gradually began to date again, then, even wiser, she used the lessons she had acquired from that bad experience to make better choices. The next time, she was determined that she would choose love with both her heart and her mind. It worked. It took over twelve years, but she married a man so perfect for her that her days rang with joy and happiness.

"It feels so good to have a trusted companion," she admitted. "It's worth the wait."

Had she allowed a setback, albeit a very serious one, sidetrack her, she would have missed what she now calls "the best, happiest days I've ever known."

That evening with Tom Sneva and his words of wisdom have stuck with me. He dropped a piece of wisdom into my heart that has bloomed and grown like a bouquet of mistletoe. I've turned it over in my mind for years, knowing that he was right: When a major setback hits us, it becomes a dividing line in our lives. Our future days will either be better for that setback or bitter for it. Had Sneva given up, he would have missed holding his dream in his hand and would have spent the rest of his life, holding it only in his heart and mind.

Don't let a setback keep you from winning again. Instead, use that setback and the strength you gain from it to find your way to winning bigger than you would have won without it. Like Sneva and my friend who found a terrific husband after a disastrous first marriage, our greatest victories usually come after our scariest challenges. Push through because better days are waiting on the other side.

CHAPTER 13:

Don't Worry About What Other People Will Think

S outhern mothers spend a lot of time—too much time, if
you ask me—worrying about what other people will think.
Appearances, to them, are important, which is why most
Southern women won't leave the house without a bit of
mascara and a dab of lipstick.

As far back as I can remember and until the day she died,
Mama showed her strong disapproval over something by saying,
"You're not going to do that. What will people think?" It
seemed that too often our lives revolved around making

decisions based on what other people would think.

One of our worst arguments when I was a teenager occurred one Sunday after church when we were going out for lunch. We stopped by the house on the way to the restaurant, so I decided to change out of my Sunday dress into a pair of slacks.

"Absolutely not," Mama exclaimed, fury rising in her voice. "People will think you didn't go to church. You're wearin' your dress, and I'm here to tell you that."

I suppose that big fight was the beginning of my not worrying excessively over what people will think. You can't control it. They're going to think whatever they want, so you're only adding unnecessary stress by fretting over it. Do the best you can and focus on what you can control. I knew I'd been to church that morning. Why did it matter if people—whom I didn't even know—questioned it? *If* they even thought to question it.

There came a time when I stood up to Mama on this and fought back even harder than I had at fifteen. When I wrote my first book, I told an entertaining story about my eccentric grandmother who toted a shotgun around the house. She answered a knock at the door by holding her shotgun in a ready-to-shoot stance. She was constantly shooting through her roof, convinced that "them men" were walking on the roof at night, trying to "drive me crazy." In truth, the crackling noise she heard was the cooling down of her tin roof after a day in the hot sun. But she couldn't be convinced. She stood ready to defend herself, so she even sat on the sofa and read the newspaper with the shotgun cradled in her lap.

That was Daddy's mother but, nonetheless, Mama took offense. She was greatly alarmed when she read the story and called me immediately. "I'm gonna pinch your head off," she began, using a familiar line to show her aggravation. "I cannot believe that you told that."

"Why? It's true."

"I don't care. You should be ashamed."

"She's been dead for twenty years. And, again, it's true."

"I know it's true," she admitted. "But it sounds awful. I'm worried. What will people think?"

Having long learned by that point to turn a scolding by Mama into humor, I shot back, "Look Mama, what you need to be worried about is what I'm gonna write when *you're* dead." I waited a beat. "And right now, it's not looking so good."

From that day forward, I either shrugged off or laughed away her worries about the opinions and thoughts of other people. I made up my mind that I would live my life as smartly as I could, focusing on my own business and not fretting over people minding my business. It hurts, of course, if we hear harsh judgments or unkind criticisms of our choices or circumstances, but the truth is that every person has erred along the way. Every family has a dysfunction or a skeleton in the closet; every person has mistakes that he wishes he could wipe away. And everyone faces setbacks in this life. Everyone.

In these times of economic troubles when jobs are lost and foreclosures are almost a norm, don't worry about what other people are saying about your situation. Put your blinders on and look straight ahead to fixing things and getting back on track. Time wasted on the opinions of others is time that could be used effectively in resolving problems more quickly.

Some people believe in Karma. Others believe that you reap what you sow. However you believe it happens, this is true: What you put out into the universe—good or bad—comes back to you. That's why you shouldn't worry excessively about the untamed tongues of others. It will come back to them.

I know two people who always enjoyed passing around gossip as a pastime. One woman, who had been contently married for years, particularly delighted in sharing news of the marital woes of others and was condescending about those who suffered, especially when it involved infidelity. One day the tables turned and she found her once flawless marriage at the center of unfaithfulness. The other woman had also participated in sharing whatever gossip came her way. She worked in an industry where everyone knew each other, so she'd get on the phone and share the latest "news."

This went on for years until she became the center of the wheel of news. She was fired suddenly from a long-term job, then spent two years cleaning houses to pay her bills. Her former colleagues were stunned by the turn of events, so she was often discussed whenever they gathered. When she eventually landed on her feet again—because better days always return—she had repented of such ways.

"I learned my lesson," she acknowledged. "After I went through that, it cured me of talking about others. It doesn't feel good when you're on the other side. It's painful." Admirably, she has stayed true to that vow.

Becky, beautiful and popular in high school, fell in love with a guy who was not only several years older but also previously married and often the subject of beauty-shop gossip. "Wild as a buck," declared the old ladies who gathered weekly for shampoo-and-sets. Becky was every parent's dream child. She had never rebelled in any way. When she announced she would marry him, the news spread like wildfire with most people pronouncing harsh judgments. The old ladies clucked their tongues and talked for weeks of how Becky was ruining her life.

"She'll rue the day she married him," they concurred. Becky stubbornly stood her ground and defied her parents' pleas while turning a deaf ear to the "expert" opinions. She proved to be just what the man needed—a good woman to love him. He straightened up and became an outstanding husband, dedicated father, and, as a businessman, a pillar of the community. Thirty-five years have proven that the change he made isn't a lark.

Once I watched an older, divorced woman torn between "what people will say" and her heart. A younger man had feverishly pursued her and, despite her misgivings, he would not give up. She fell in love, and it was easy to see why. He was adorable in every way especially in how he doted on her. Still, she refused to marry him, worried over the opinions of others. Also she was concerned that he would wind up having to take care of her in old age. We all encouraged her to avoid pleasing others and follow her heart. The critics were living her life. Why should they have a say in it?

Finally, after years of courtship, she gave in to her heart and married him. They stayed married for almost forty years until death did them part. In an ironic twist, it was him who died first and she who nursed him through years of cancer. Had she listened to others, she would have missed out on the happiest years of her life. Though she was, at first, swayed by the judgments of others, she eventually stood up boldly and turned a deaf ear to their worthless words. It led to her bravest and best decision.

When times are hard and troubling, fret not over what others are thinking or saying. It will only add unnecessary stress and take focus away from finding a resolution to your problems.

If you're facing a decision that pertains to your life, make the best choice possible based on instinct, information, and heart. Don't, though, allow what other people will think to sway your choices.

It could cost you stress and, possibly, a loss of tremendous happiness.

CHAPTER 14:

Emotions Will Trick You into Making Bad Decisions

Over the years I have said many things I regretted, some were regretted the moment they escaped my mouth and I frantically hoped against hope that I could retrieve them. A few comments have gone so far as to haunt me for years, words that bring a tiny wave of nausea when recalled. But I have never regretted anything that I held back and did not say. Learning to ride shotgun over emotion and use common sense, instead, will save a lot of heartache.

When I was eleven and misbehaving over something, Daddy

used a well-known threat of parents, "We'll just see what Santa Claus has to say about that."

I knew better than to say it. I should have held my tongue, but I couldn't help myself. I twisted my face into a defiant look and retorted, "There *is* no Santa Claus!" It felt good to say it for two seconds, but almost instantly, the good feeling was replaced by a thump in my heart. In trying to call Daddy's hand, I had made a costly mistake.

Daddy's eyes widened and a grin slid across his face. "Oh? Is that right? Well, we'll just see what happens now."

Apparently, Santa Claus's feelings were hurt over my disbelief, especially after all the years he had been so good and kind to me. He never visited again. There's no telling how many Christmas gifts that little slip of the tongue cost me. It was an expensive wisecrack. Words and actions cannot be taken back and some, triggered by emotion, can never be made right.

One of the biggest enemies we face in day-to-day life is that of our own emotions. Desperation, fear, loneliness—even love if it's with an insincere person—can drive us to choices for which we will pay later down the road. "Don't ever go out on a first date with someone you wouldn't want to marry," Mama used to say. When you're eighteen or even twenty-five that doesn't seem like advice worth paying a lot of attention to, but few words are truer. We always think that we control our emotions, but emotions tend to rule us. If you don't choose carefully who you date the first time, then you open the door to marrying the wrong person and making a lot of trouble for yourself.

"You might go out with someone and think it's just fun," Mama explained. "Then, before you know it, you're in love and you can't make yourself walk away."

A friend of mine did just that. She was popular and often

had her choice of guys. She fell into the habit of dating "for fun," which was easy for her since there were always several guys around, wanting a date. We began to notice she was dating one guy more than others and, after a while, she was dating only him. In a short time, they were engaged and everyone was puzzled. He was handsome, nice, funny, and hard-working but they had little in common. It was one of those marriages where someone would say, "She married *him?*"

Yes, she did. Emotion got involved and swayed her common sense. She was attracted and excited by him, so she looked past differences in education, ambition, upbringing, financial discipline, religious practices, and basic principles. When the passion died down, so did the marriage. It was five years of their lives that neither can get back, and in breaking up, it hurt much more later than it would have hurt to split while dating. If people dated without getting intimately involved, there would be fewer marriages and fewer failures. The emotion of passion can move the earth and not always in a good way.

Another friend, due to religious convictions, chose to abstain from an intimate relationship until she married. She met, who we all believed (and of course, our opinions mattered greatly), someone who seemed perfect for her. They were compatible in many ways, but it turned out he had a temper that he seemed to display only with her.

But she loved him mightily and wanted to spend her life with him. For a while, she overlooked the angry outbursts and mean digs. To herself, she made excuses and believed she could love him out of such behavior. Love is strong, but, on its own, it cannot solve some problems like abuse, drug addiction, alcoholism, or anger.

One day, furious over something relatively minor, he called

and left a blistering voice mail on her phone. Word of caution: Be careful with e-mails and voice mails. They can become powerful enemies because they can be replayed and reread. Repeatedly.

I had long reminded her, "The best a man ever treats you is *before* he marries you. It doesn't get better, only worse." She decided to give him an ultimatum: to draw a line and lay her cards on the table. She would not marry him unless and until his behavior was corrected. Because they were not having an intimate relationship, she was more in control of her feelings than she would have been otherwise. Through counseling and determination by both, they were able to work it out. But left alone, the problem would have only grown and festered. Emotions can trick you into letting others, even the ones who love you, pound on your self-esteem. Keep those emotions in check so that you protect your confidence and self-esteem.

"Be careful what you tell your best friend," was another one of Mama's constant admonishments. "She may not always be your best friend." Ohhhh, that makes a lot of sense. On those real-life crime shows, criminals are always winding up in jail because they confided in the wrong person. Don't you just want to say, "What were you thinking?" There again, emotions. Someone needs someone to talk to and, at the right moment, it is shared with someone who turns out to be the wrong person.

One day, one of my friends was in her office, caught up completely in work when the phone rang. She answered and the woman said, "You don't know me, but I know something you need to know." For the next ten minutes, the stranger proceeded to tell her that her husband had been having an affair for months. She was loaded with details—the name of the woman, where she worked, where they met, and how often. She told where he hid his car and even knew the excuses that the husband gave to the wife on his whereabouts. As it turned out, it was all true. The whistle-blower was—get this—the best friend of the mistress. The two had a serious falling out over some trivial matter, so the "best friend" decided to get even and share her friend's confidences. You never know when your confidante will turn out to be untrustworthy.

Sometimes we have bad days or hard times because we participated in the creation of them—buy a car that's too expensive, marry the wrong person, quit a job in a burst of anger, go on an eating binge after getting bad news, try cocaine "just once" and so on. These kinds of decisions are fueled by emotions that will trick us into doing what feels good at the moment rather than looking at what is best for the long term. You can actively participate in creating better days by making wise choices, ones that aren't overly influenced by emotions.

It will certainly save a lot of heartbreak and tears.

CHAPTER 15:

Sometimes Our Greatest Blessings Arrive Disguised as Heartaches

Her voice softened to a whisper as she talked about those days, the ones that almost broke her. And they probably would have, had she not been young, physically strong, and emotionally resilient. When Aunt Ozelle recalled those tribulations back in 1937, her feeble voice crackled with both age and emotion. With over seventy years having disappeared into vapor, the grief still lingered but wisdom had covered it like moss on a riverbank.

"It's a wonder we made it out alive," she said, sighing. "But lookin' back, it turned out to be a good thing. The Lord knowed what he was doin'. Otherwise, we'd never left the mountains."

In those days in the Appalachian foothills, the poor were really poor, their backbones hollow from lack of food, and their brows heavy with the kind of worry that will drive a man to an early grave. While a severe Depression had changed the comfort level of most, it had paralyzed many in rural America and the mountains. It wasn't just a matter of keeping a roof over their heads, for there were days they did not know where they would find their next meal. Farms were lost, babies died from lack of medical care, and crops dried up in the field for lack of rain. Out of those dark days would emerge a remarkable breed of people who would never be bowed by adversity again, people who could look a challenge in the eye and not blink, survivors who could go toe-to-toe with whatever the devil threw their way and come out the winner. Like gold that is refined by fire, those who struggled through the uncertain days of the Great Depression were made better for the experience.

Daddy was about nine years old when he lost fifty cents in a bank that closed. He never forgot it. When he grew up, he kept his cash in a safe deposit box "just in case." He could not be dissuaded by the argument that the money was insured now if a bank failed. He had been burned once, so he lived accordingly from that day forward. That's not a bad thing. When we learn from difficulties, we can avoid similar situations in the future.

Aunt Ozelle, Mama's oldest sister, had married the handsome Tom, whom she had met at church. Just sixteen, she was ready to be a wife, having been raised to work hard and do whatever it took. They took up residence in a little rented house on a tiny farm and set about the business of trying to survive. In their first three years of marriage, things went from bad to worse until they were plopped down in the middle of 1937 and regardless of how hard President Franklin D. Roosevelt was trying to rescue the starving South, help wasn't coming quick enough for Tom and Ozelle. Foxes ate all their chickens. Their milk cow—the one that Ozelle's daddy had given them as a wedding present—had caught her head between a post and the floor, strangling her to death and taking their milk and butter supply. Coming back from the barn where she had discovered the dead cow, a nine-months pregnant Ozelle dropped to her knees to pray.

"I prayed that God's will be done, whatever that was," she remembered. The next day the baby arrived, stillborn.

"I couldn't be angry with God and I wasn't. I asked that His will be done."

Thirteen months later, a healthy baby boy was born but died two months later from pneumonia.

"I carried the greatest burden in my heart, but looking back, I know God knew what he was doin'. I don't know how we would have fed those children. Times were so hard."

It was time to go, time to leave the only home they had ever known. For mountain people, it's hard to step outside of that cocoon of familiarity. It's why so many in the deep reaches of the Appalachians are stuck in an ongoing cycle of poverty. They'd rather stick with what they know—meager and uncomfortable as it is—rather than venture out into a bold, fast-moving world. For those who are brave enough to escape, it is a great accomplishment and one that should not be underestimated for the courage it took.

Uncle Tom and Aunt Ozelle packed up their few possessions and headed down from the mountains into Gainesville, thirty-five miles away but light years removed from the way of life they had known. It was the beginning of a better day that came and stayed for the reminder of their long lives. Uncle Tom, hard-working and solid, found a good job. Later, when World War II came, they reached into their arsenal of courage and struck out for Newport News, Virginia, where he got a job in the naval yard. After the war, they came back to Gainesville and set about making the kind of life they would never have had in the mountains. They took in an orphaned child who joined their two children. Uncle Tom took a job as a salesman for a wholesale food company and carefully managed every penny he made. Aunt Ozelle was a prudent spender, too, because once you've done without, you never want to be in that place again, so you save with an eye toward a rainy day.

Both lived well into their nineties and, throughout their lives, always believed that the best had been born out of the worst. Months before she died, Aunt Ozelle and I sat on the screened-in front porch of the cozy bungalow that they had bought when the war ended. It was a new house then with indoor plumbing and the kind of comfortable abode that they would never have had in the mountains. After all, that region did not have electricity until midway through the war. A beautiful, enormous magnolia stood tall, strong, and healthy, with its limbs spread out to cover the entire yard and arched over the house.

"I have never seen such a gorgeous magnolia," I commented. "The shape of the tree is remarkable."

She eyed it for a moment and nodded. "It was just a little seedling when we bought this house. There must be water running under its roots because it's always grown fast."

That tree symbolizes the lives of the people who lived there—over the years, like that tree, their family grew strong and healthy. Their roots had found the water necessary to nourish their lives. In the mountains, their thirst could not be quenched.

Their story speaks to the hard times of today and the interruption that many discovered during an economic upheaval. Had Uncle Tom and Aunt Ozelle not experienced brutal times, they would not have been forced into action that produced the best lives possible. Both readily admitted that if it had been possible to stay in the mountains and survive, they would have done it. Adversity delivers some of our greatest gifts, but we have to let go of the past and what was in order to find what can be.

When I lost a well-paying job in a corporate downsizing, I was numb with worry. Recently divorced, I had a mortgage and car payment. Also my father was dying, so I couldn't move to another town for a job. Quiet despair was a constant companion. It took everything within my being to keep worry and anxiety at bay. Things worked out, though. Better than I ever imagined. I took my skills and experience and became a consultant. I landed a contract that paid more and gave me the flexibility to help my parents and to work toward my childhood dream of being an author. Nothing could pay me to go back through those months of being scared with worry but, on the other hand, I wouldn't take a million dollars for what that downturn delivered.

Because my life was upended and I was forced to find a new path, my life went from being ordinary to being extraordinary. Just like Uncle Tom and Aunt Ozelle. Without the adversity, my life would be much poorer indeed. Because of it, my life has been enriched with experience, adventure, and satisfaction. Of course, if you had asked me at the time, I would have been a coward and cried out, "I don't care what comes from this. Just get me out of this now!"

No doubt you can look back at your own adversities and see blessings that resulted from that journey. Nothing is ever completely bad. When hard times come, trust that right behind them will come better times. Resist the urge to dwell on what has soured and look forward with happy anticipation to what will come as a result. A blessing lies just around the corner.

CHAPTER 16:

Worry Not Over What Hard Work and Money Can Replace

I looked at the wreckage of what had been my childhood home, the bungalow I bought after Mama's death and turned into my office. Now, it was laid to waste, flooded by a water line that had broken and run unrestrained for days. It resembled not at all the home where love and security had abounded for many years of my life, where laughter rang out, where Mama often used her apron to dry my tears, or where Daddy sat in the den each night, reading either the newspaper or his worn, black Bible.

The destruction stunned me. Soggy ceilings had fallen, leaving a mountain of tattered drywall and pieces of insulation across the rooms. Water ran over my shoes, making a rushing stream that flowed directly into the heating and air vents. Mama's favorite recliner was ruined, and that club chair that they had begun marriage with, when money was so scarce that they could not afford a lamp (and would not own one for the first decade of their marriage), was beyond being salvaged.

Since Mama's death, ten years after Daddy said his final good-bye on that night lit by a full moon, I had clung tenaciously to anything that had been hers, his, or theirs. Anything that his fingers had touched or her heart had cherished had paramount importance to me. I especially clung to the remnants of Mama's earthly existence. I needed it all to feel her presence close to me and to have her comfort me as she so often did when the trials of my life were overwhelming. It was there she had taught, "No matter what comes your way, look it in the eye and stare it down." When she died, I bought the house, keeping everything as she had left it, but, suddenly, all I owned was one big, overwhelming mess. The loss was enormous. There at my feet laid debris that had been the props in a lifetime of memories. Many possessions that I treasured had been drowned, broken, and destroyed. They existed no more.

But I did not cry.

For as clearly as I could hear the clinking of Mama's biscuit pan on the stove top, I could hear the strong, reasonable voice of my daddy saying, "Kid, worry not over what hard work and money can replace."

As heartbroken as I felt, I had my health, my loved ones were well, and there were numerous other blessings. Given the choice between the loss of possessions, even precious sentimental ones, or the loss of my health or the death of a loved one, there would be no choice. I would choose exactly what happened. Of course, we aren't given choices in these matters, but it does help to remember that the things that can be replaced by hard work aren't worth a second worry.

When the economy took a hard downturn, I watched my friends lose their jobs, their homes to foreclosure, and even their businesses. One friend and her husband had been successful real estate developers, often turning huge pieces of land into expensive subdivisions. Like many, they were caught short-handed on cash when the real estate market plummeted. For almost two years, they struggled to make monthly interest payments in the tens of thousands of dollars. They sold everything they could sell from furniture to jewelry to cars because they sure couldn't sell a house or a piece of land. The moment that one payment was turned over to the bank, they began worrying about the next one. There was no peace of mind. Finally, there was nothing left to sell. They had to face the inevitable: They were about to lose everything. There would be nothing to show for twenty years of work. One morning, they drove to the bank to take the keys to unsold houses and signed over a major piece of land worth millions. It was over. They had lost everything except for their clothes and four rooms of furniture.

With nowhere to go, a family member offered her grandparents' old farmhouse. Gratefully, they took it, even though it was a long way from the manor that had once been home. This isn't a sad story, though, because they're happier than ever.

"We love it!" she exclaimed. "It's like the weight of the world lifted off our shoulders. It's a simple life, and we're just as

105

happy as we can be." They buy and sell vintage merchandise, and it's plenty enough to keep their simple life going.

"We would never have chosen this, but now we would not choose to go back," she said. "It's the happiest we've been in many years. We've got our health, each other, and a roof over our heads. We're in good shape." She smiled. "If we want to, we can roll up our sleeves and earn it back. Right now, we'll pass on that because we like life just like it is."

As the economy has shaken some to the very core, many are embarrassed at the loss of worldly goods. There's no need to be. Don't be concerned with what others think of your financial position. Most of those people you're worried about are worried about how they're going to make next month's mortgage payment. They're so concerned with meeting their obligations that they have no time to think about others who aren't making ends meet. Without question, whenever they pass a foreclosed house in their neighborhood, they whisper a prayer to spare them from the same fate. When you're worrying about what other people think about your hard times, then you're taking your attention away from correcting those troubles. Every person goes through trying times. Tribulations are not reserved for just a few. They're the birthright of everyone who lives long enough.

For whatever reason, bad things always have varying amounts of good tucked into them. Though I lost many precious items, there were still some important pieces left like flowerpots that Daddy had crafted for Mama out of old cast-iron kettles. With the help of insurance, I set about restoring the house and, in the bargain, decided to remodel. I took out walls to open it up, added a new kitchen, updated the bathroom, and added new wood floors. It turned out pretty and was such a blessing, one that I was forced to find because of the flood damage. Now enthused over what hard work and money had replaced, I set about decorating.

One afternoon, I brought in a dozen bags filled with linens, bathroom accessories, and such. In a hurry to leave for an out-of-town wedding, I left the bags on the floor. Two days later I returned and stopped by the house. The moment I pulled in, a sick feeling of dread hit my stomach. Something wasn't right. I could feel that someone had been there. I jumped from the car and flew to the door. Before I opened it, I looked through the window. Everything was gone. Stolen. Furniture had been moved, so that rugs could be taken. Cabinet doors were open and cleaned out. All that remained were the pieces too heavy to move quickly.

Every sentimental piece that had survived the flood had been stolen, including Daddy's handmade flowerpots. For the second time in a few months, I had to remind myself not to worry over what hard work and money can replace. Honestly, I didn't shrug it off. It hurt. It gnawed a hole in my heart as I thought of thieves who had taken what was dear to me and would sell it for a few dollars to people who wouldn't think twice of the history and memories involved.

Hard days happen and when they do, we have to dig down deep and find the strength to get us through to a better day. Time passes and things that once hurt do not matter anymore. After a few months, I couldn't recall exactly what all had been taken except for the flowerpots.

There was still good in all that bad. My break-in led to the breakup of a major burglary ring, and while I got nothing back, others did and the criminals went to jail. The house, which I would never have touched or changed if the flood had not forced my hand, became my office and an adorable place that I could offer to others in time of temporary need. When we are blessed, it is our responsibility to share with others in their time of need. Good was found in the ashes of what had been.

Of course, some family heirlooms were lost forever but as Mama always reminded us, "You have to take the bad with the good." The gift comes in taking the good with appreciation and shrugging off the bad. It all begins with realizing that material possessions can be replaced. Wouldn't you rather have someone you can kiss than something you can buy with a dollar?

Can you put a price on how much you'd take for your sight, hearing, or a leg? I betcha there is not enough money in the world to buy any of that from you. Would you give up your house over giving up the life of your child? Absolutely. Keep it all in perspective and just keep moving.

My friend Poet is a common man's philosopher who always has a wise take on any situation. Once, we were discussing someone who was in critical condition after a massive stroke. The prognosis, should he live, was grim.

"Death isn't always the worst thing that can happen to us," I commented solemnly.

"No, it's not," Poet shot back quickly. "The worst thing that can happen is to go broke and live forever."

Truer words could never be spoken.

CHAPTER 17:

Without Risk, the Joy and Excitement of Life Disappears

How many people do you know—especially those who have passed forty—who are enthused and happy about jumping out of bed every morning? What about you? Do you ever wake up with that excited pit in your stomach about the anticipation of the day and its events? If you've forgotten that feeling, think back to the days of your teenage years when you spent days or weeks happily anticipating a forthcoming date, trip, or occasion. Remember how much fun it was to joyously plan for an event?

Several years ago, a friend asked me if I was dating anyone special. I shook my head. "No, I date regularly, but it's been a long time since I dated anyone I was excited about getting dressed up for."

My spontaneous response was so uncannily accurate that my friend often repeated it to people whenever discussions about dating arose. During college whenever I was dating someone who thrilled my heart, I would spend a week planning and shopping for my outfit. On the day of our date, I'd start dressing hours before he arrived. I spent a remarkable amount of time on my hair, paying exacting attention to every strand and applying makeup with careful precision. When I finished, I'd twirl in front of the full-length mirror, scrutinizing every inch. By the time my friend asked that question, it had come to a point where I was bored with the guys I dated. I dressed from head to toe in thirty minutes or less, barely glanced in the mirror, and hurried on. When I did eventually meet someone who brought back that excitement, it was a treasure.

The hazard is that we can reach that point with everything in our lives—jobs, personal relationships, home, or family. There comes a point, as years pass, where it is natural to drift toward comfortable and safe. Life can wear you out with its challenges, unpredictability, and stresses. As we grow older, we "reward" ourselves by choosing comfortable and predictable over new and untried. Aw, we so enjoy that for a while. It's easier to work with the same people every day because you've come to know what to expect. It's simpler to have toast for breakfast each morning rather than choose from a variety of cereals. It's mindless behavior. Safe and comfortable, though, have expiration dates on the contentment they bring. Before you realize it, being comfortable and staying within the same confines on a daily basis is boring. And boring eats up joy and excitement like Pac-Man gobbles up enemies. When gleeful anticipation is lost, then life becomes drudgery, which then is a quick walk over to melancholy, and from there it's a hop, skip, and a jump into mild or deep depression that can stretch through the remainder of life. This kind of behavior scares away better days.

Keeping risk-taking in life protects our five senses so that we can truly feel and live. Do you remember a time when you fell head-over-heels in love? Suddenly, the colors of the world looked brighter, food tasted better, your laughter came quicker, and your step was lighter. That's because you were taking a risk. You were putting your heart out there, throwing caution to the wind and taking a chance. The same rules apply in everyday life, whether it's business or pleasure. When you step out of the box of comfort and security that you've come to love, your senses are awakened and you are jolted back to life.

There are three kinds of risks: calculated, crazy, and stupid. Calculated risk is when you weigh all the possible outcomes and see that while risk of failure is there, it's minimal and the upside could produce enjoyment. An example is purchasing your dream home where the mortgage payment is 40 percent more than rent, but you've crunched the numbers and know you can swing it if you're careful with your budget. You have savings tucked away that, after the down payment, you'll still have three or four house payments in the event that a financial setback occurs. The upside is that you'll own your dream home and be investing in it regularly.

Crazy risk is spontaneous. It's "Hey, let's do this." It provides a quick, intense high. With calculated risk, your senses are heightened and enlivened, but with crazy risk, your adrenals soar, your heart beats quicker, and you excel with joy. Stepping into crazy risk as opposed to calculated is like moving from the lumbering family sedan on a highway into a fast-moving sports car on the interstate where you zip in and out of traffic. I once took a crazy risk, one that had everyone speechless, yet it has proven to be one of my greatest adventures.

When Princess Diana died, I decided on a whim to go to London for the funeral. It was spontaneous and exciting but certainly stepping out of a safe place for me. I couldn't talk any of my friends into joining the adventure, so I booked a flight, reserved a hotel, and began to pack. Everyone was in disbelief that I would travel alone just to be close to an historical event yet most people thought I was bold, brave, and spirited. One of those "most people" was not my mother. She was livid.

"That is the craziest thing I have ever heard of. I forbid you to do such a stupid thing. It's dangerous and lacks good sense."

"I'm going," I replied. I was old enough to make my own decisions and had the money to do it. It was a crazy risk. I was traveling internationally and would be in a city packed to the gills with extra people, so something could have happened. My heart stirred deeply and beckoned me onward. I had been following the Princess, her fashion, and generosity for years. I wanted to see the funeral procession in person. It was crazy because it was spur-of-the-moment and it was a big step outside the box of normality. I had never done anything like it before.

That crazy risk paid off beautifully. The moment I boarded the plane, I declared my adult independence from my mother. We all want to please our parents and have them approve of our decisions. We want their support. But that isn't always going to happen. For the first time, I defied my mother and followed my own desires. It was exhilarating. I had been out of college for ten years, but finally I *owned* my life. It was the beginning of a new self-assured adulthood for me because I discovered I was competent in managing decisions. I returned home with increased self-worth, proud of my boldness.

I also learned the value of memories and of tasting life, not just watching it roll by. I would have seen more of the funeral on television at home than I saw from the crowd, but I felt the air of the September Saturday that was free of humidity with a slight breeze ruffling the trees. I experienced the sadness and the tears of her admirers and the quiet streets packed with people who did not murmur or whisper as the horse-drawn casket passed by. I met two young guys on the Tube, who grabbed my hand and said, "Come with us. We know exactly where to go for the best view." Then, they sweetly pushed me in front of them when the casket approached so that I could see it best. Later, we went to a park where the funeral was played on an enormous theater screen and sat on the ground with thousands of others.

On that trip, I met a young lawyer from New York City, who became a friend. We toured the floral tributes at Kensington Palace that were at least four feet high and spent hours reading the notes that people had posted on the walls. As the day ended, we sat in the park under an enormous, ancient tree and talked of our aspirations. I left with a heart full of memories and a tongue full of stories to tell.

It was a crazy risk. I admitted it then and I affirm it now. But it was one of the best decisions I ever made. The success of that decision gave me the courage and confidence to take other crazy risks in the years that have passed since then. Mama even got over being mad at me. She had declared in our last conversation before I headed to the airport, "I won't be telling anyone about this because I don't want anyone to know what a crazy daughter I raised. I'm embarrassed."

I ended up on national television, though, when one of the networks interviewed me about being an American who had flown across the ocean just for the funeral. Mama saw it. So, did most of her friends and all the folks at church. When I got home, she was buzzing around happily, asking for details. I eyed her warily. "What's going on? You told me you didn't want anyone to know this."

"I know," she replied cheerfully. "But then everyone at church saw you on television, and they all were so impressed and thought it was great." She smiled beatifically. "So, now, I think it's great, too!"

A stupid risk is jumping out of a four-story high window expecting to fly like a bird or placing the deed to a fully paid mortgage on a high stakes black jack table. It's kissing your best friend's spouse, thinking it will be meaningless and won't lead to anything. It's running naked in a winter's blizzard while still on the mend from double pneumonia. Sometimes stupid risks can sneak up on you, so be diligent in watching for them because no good ever comes from a stupid risk.

The worse kind of risk, though, is ceasing to take risk at all. Playing it safe is boring and hazardous to your health because the lack of excitement will slowly kill your spirit and soul—then the body begins to follow. Avoid stupid but make calculated and crazy risks a part of your life. You'll laugh more and enjoy life with a soul-satisfying fullness and, in the bargain, you'll coax better days into your grasp.

CHAPTER 18:

Courage Comes by Choice and Not by Chance

I doubt that anyone was ever born brave. It is a conditioning, a mindset, a deliberate decision. We either choose to be courageous or we choose to let life and its trying circumstances beat us down. We have the opportunity to choose between courage and fear, whether it is standing up to financial terrors, looking cancer in the eye and staring it down, or fighting to overcome injustices or misfortunes.

The moment I met him, the pure memory of it, has been tucked away in my mind for years. Though what I would come to learn from him was extraordinary, the moment of our introduction was not. As a sports writer, still in college, I worked part-time at the daily newspaper. At the end of every summer, I would interview local high school football players then write a preview of the team's talent for the upcoming season in a special sports section. Jim Lofton, a tough but likeable and fair man, was the head coach of East Hall High School. When I asked him to direct me to three or four of his best players for interviews, he rattled off three names, including a defensive tackle named Andrew Goudelock.

Andrew came off the field that day, walking toward me in a stream of bright sunlight, his face mostly obscured by the light until he came within a few feet. I saw that a dark tint of somberness clung to his face but when I offered my hand, he shook it and smiled, a row of glistening white teeth flashing against his smooth, dark chocolate-colored skin. His answers were typical of a shy teenager—"yes," "no," "I guess"—plus, I had discovered that the teenage players either had a fascination with or a wariness of a girl sports writer who was not much older than them.

Andrew was wary.

It is fair to say that we would never have become close friends, certainly not the confidantes that we became, had it not been for what happened two weeks later. At a routine physical, given free to the players by a local doctor, a suspicious mass was discovered in his left knee. Tests revealed that the sixteen-year-old had bone cancer. Before any of us could absorb the news, Andrew was whisked away to an Atlanta hospital where his leg was amputated above the knee. Being a sports reporter isn't all fun and games. Sometimes you have to cover a story like Andrew's cancer. It was the first heart-wrenching story of my career, one widely read by an audience touched by the courage and character that Andrew and his beautiful mother, Katherine, possessed.

For whatever reason, Andrew's wariness of me melted into trust and friendship. He took to calling me at home two or three nights a week, and, occasionally, he would send letters penned in his small, tight handwriting. Don't get the impression that Andrew talked a lot. He did not. Our phone calls often consisted of me doing much of the talking intertwined with large amounts of silence on Andrew's part. I came to know that he simply needed the comfort of a friend close by, especially on the nights that his mama was working at a department store. The night's quiet, it seemed, brought out a new uneasiness after he lost his leg. Often, I would answer the phone, hear his soft "hey," then fling myself onto my bed and talk until he decided to end the call.

"You're so brave," I said one night.

"Naw," he replied. "I can't change things and get my leg back. I wish I could." Like most high school athletes, he had dreamed of playing college ball then advancing into the pros. "I ain't got no choice."

Andrew, though, did have a choice. He could have laid down, given up, and felt sorry for himself, but, instead, he chose to fight back. He returned to school despite the sickness brought on by chemotherapy and began to inspire many by his refusal to accept self-pity and even stronger refusal to be hailed as a hero. When the school decided to honor him with Andrew Goudelock Day, including an assembly in the gym where he was to be awarded various commendations, he called and asked if I would attend.

"I certainly will!" I wanted to be there as a friend, but I was also assigned as a reporter to cover it.

He paused before continuing. "Will you sit by me?"

"Andrew, I would love to," I replied, touched by how far our friendship had come. "But your mama and Coach Lofton should sit by you. I'll be close, though. Don't worry about that."

That day, after the honors and words, Andrew rose slowly from his chair on the gym floor, wrestled his crutches under his arms, and hobbled over to the microphone. I knew it was hard for him. Hundreds of students, faculty, and others had gathered to show their love and support but Andrew was painfully shy and intensely modest. Quietly, he whispered, "Thank you."

Aw, but the greatest inspiration was still to come. The following spring before Andrew became a junior, he told me a secret. "I'm gonna play again."

"What?" I was puzzled. Andrew played tackle, but he could barely walk with only one leg. How could he play again?

His tone was firm, filled with resolve. "I'm gonna tell Coach Lofton." So he did and then he did. It was a clear, cold Friday night, the kind where warm breath hangs visibly in the air when Coach Lofton put Andrew in to play. All those who knew Andrew as well as the opposing team watched as he hopped on one leg out on the field. Determinedly, he lined up in position. The ball snapped and Andrew lost no time leaping toward his man. He pushed with all his might while the player, who outweighed him by twenty or thirty pounds and had both legs, tried to push back. For several seconds, while other players fell around him, Andrew held his ground before his opponent managed to push him down. The crowd stood and cheered as Andrew, refusing help from anyone, lifted himself from the ground and hopped back off the field without glancing once toward the applauding, admiring crowd.

That was just the beginning. He continued to fight and to play. He worked out regularly with the team, used weights to build his upper body, and readjusted his dreams from that of being a player to being a coach. Setbacks, either serious or minor, may call for a readjustment to the vision of our dreams, but they seldom call for an end to them. Obstacles are a part of the journey. We will always face them but, like Andrew, we must avoid self-pity and remap the route. There is no dead end to any dream or ambition, so when you get to what looks like the end of the road, make a U-turn and travel back toward another road.

When his senior year came, he earned a spot on Georgia's All-Star team, this after having played through multiple surgeries and the grim news that the cancer, once abated, had returned and spread to his lungs. That night of the All-Star game, he was introduced, then an entire stadium rose to give him a five-minute ovation. Characteristically, Andrew pursed his lips, looked down, and shook his head.

About a year later, I was at my desk at *USA Today*, where I was working on loan from my newspaper, when my phone rang. "I hate to call you like this," Mama began, a tone of sadness coating her words. "But I have some bad news. Andrew died yesterday." He was nineteen years old and had valiantly battled cancer for almost four years.

Deeply grieved, I pushed back the tears and wrote my last tribute to my young friend—his obituary. His legacy, though, will never die. It is one of courage chosen, the mightiest kind of courage. Andrew's dreams were seemingly destroyed at a young, innocent age, yet he had the wisdom of someone far older. He picked up the pieces of his dreams and put them together in a new vision. Through it all, he inspired more people in four years than most inspire during a long life of living. He refused to take the easy way out. He did not give up. He chose courage, covered himself in it like a suit of armor and fought the toughest battle any warrior can face.

In NASCAR, I worked with legendary racer, Bobby Allison. His son, Davey, was a friend and contemporary of mine. Bobby, who was undeniably one of the sport's greats, knew tremendous success and happiness in life, but there came a turning point, a period of time, when sorrow was a constant companion. It began with a terrible crash at Pocono International Raceway in which Bobby suffered a serious head injury that ended his career and almost ended his life. A few years later, his son, Clifford, was killed in a racecar accident in Michigan, then eleven months later, Davey died after a helicopter crash. In almost a blink of an eye, he had lost both sons. Later, he and his wife divorced, and he faced financial challenges.

I ran into him once in Talladega and we began a conversation that turned to his boys. He reached into his back pocket, pulled out his billfold, and retrieved a photo of his two sons together, clowning around. As I looked at the photo, tears filled my eyes, and I began sniffling. It saddened me to think of the friend I had lost, but at the same time, I could not imagine how deep and profound this man's loss was. His life, it seemed to me, had crumbled and rusted around him.

"You've lost so much," I whimpered, shaking my head and wiping my eyes.

Then, something remarkable happened. This man, the one who should have been consoled by me, put his arm around my shoulders and offered me comfort. He spoke words of strength and wisdom, words I shall long carry with me and not forget.

"Don't cry for me," he said, smiling. Surprised, I looked up to see a sparkle in his eyes and an undeniable determination. "You see, I'm the luckiest man God ever made." My mouth dropped. Lucky? In my eyes, this man was anything but. He explained that he had had a career that he loved, one that had made him famous. For many years, he had a wife who loved him and stood by him, a woman he loved beyond measure, and he'd had the love of two of the finest sons a man could ask for. "Sure, I've lost it all," he admitted with a slight shrug. "But at least I had it, and that's a whole lot more than most people can say. I can't do anything about what's happened. I can't bring my boys back, but I can make the best of my years left. I have to remember the good and not dwell on the bad."

I was astounded. Outside of Andrew, it was the most amazing stand of courage I had ever witnessed. Bobby refused to give his future as ransom to the past. He was determined to pick up the pieces, remember the happiness, and use it to mold a resilient future, which is exactly what he did including remarrying the love of his life. I realized right then and there that if we are to prevail over a life that sometimes seeks to defeat us, we must choose courage because courage comes by choice and not by chance. You can lie down and let life claim victory, or you can come back fighting and take the victory for yourself.

Whatever trial you face whether it's the loss of a job, another financial setback, a health concern, a relationship problem, make the choice of arming yourself with courage. If fear threatens to tiptoe into your mind or if negative thoughts abound, push them out of the way with more powerful thoughts of determination and courage. Focus on the positive. Hardships happen to each of us, but better days also happen to each of us. We have to put our heads down, steady our feet, and walk directly into the storm. When it's over—and it will be over—calm weather returns and brings with it sunny, mild days.

Life can only get the better of you, if you give into defeat and fear. Mama always said during the most trying times that we faced, "It could be worse." And though I always hated hearing that, it's the truth. The best way to find courage in difficult times is to look at the blessings that remain and remind yourself how hard life would be without those. Then, with your chin up, put on the armor of mental courage and fight back until you win, until that trial has passed and you have forged your way back to a place of contentment and happiness.

Remember: courage is a choice.

CHAPTER 19:

Adopt an Older Person and Swap Your Time for His Wisdom

One morning as I was having breakfast with a loved one, I noticed that close by was a table of elderly men, most in their eighties. Some used canes to steady their walk while others looked frail and shaky of hand. Across the country, there are daily gatherings of men like this who assemble for coffee and a light breakfast. They're retired with little to do, so they meet to discuss the weather, stock portfolios, politics, and their families. Though few bother to ask, their wealth of wisdom, especially when combined, could solve many problems.

As the morning light streamed through the windows and lighted their deeply lined faces and teeth yellowed with age, bits and pieces of their conversation drifted over to our table. On that particular morning, they were discussing the use of pesticides and what should be done to preserve the land and protect consumers. Later, they moved on to politics. Their observations were solid, honed by decades of learning. They had fought in wars, participated in the building of a strong America, and raised families. From the harvest of life, they had plucked an abundance of wisdom, learning over the long course of life what only experience teaches.

I sipped coffee and thought, "If only we younger ones were wise enough to sit at the feet of these masters of life and seek counsel, how much better equipped we would be to battle the challenges of life."

Those who have lived through a lifetime of mistakes, challenges, and triumphs can teach powerfully. If only we would take time to listen.

Gene Bobo was in his late eighties when I met him, but I knew he was a man of quality and conviction. He had been a successful businessman who turned into a conscientious philanthropist. He was elegant, wise, stately, and kind. He was also lonely, his beloved wife having died years earlier and his only child living over an hour away. My family and I adopted him. We made regular visits and phone calls to him and at least once a month dined with him. He was healthy in both body and mind well into his nineties before slipping on a wet kitchen floor and taking a terrible fall. For the last eighteen months of his life, he was relegated to a wheelchair but his mind was unbelievably bright and clear. His face lit up with delight whenever I visited, and after I settled down into a chair comfortably, he would launch into detailed recollections of his life's experiences. Without hesitation, he recalled his days in World War II in the Pacific when he, with a chemical degree from Clemson University, was assigned to chemical warfare.

"We used mustard gas," he said, explaining that it had first been used in World War I. "It would do incalculable damage to the skin." He folded his hands and cast an eye toward the ceiling. "Diethylenetriamine."

Without a stutter from his ninety-four-year-old tongue, he repeated the chemical name. "That is the key ingredient in a solution that will abate the damage of mustard gas."

He had forgotten little in a life in which he worked hard, loved devotedly, and gave much back to his community and church. My visits lifted the loneliness in his life, but our time together was more important to me than to him because he shared wisdom and experiences gained over a long life of success.

One night over dinner, I unexpectedly discovered a remarkable piece of trivia. Historical significance, really. Mr. Bobo returned home from that stint in the Pacific to work in management for a textile manufacturing company that made hosiery, known as stockings in those days of girdles and garter belts. He would eventually become president of the company. A colleague and fellow engineer named Bill Leath called Mr. Bobo with an idea of creating a stretch yarn that could be woven on circular machines like socks. Remember, there was a time when stockings were seamed together and women had the unpleasant task of constantly checking those seams to ensure they were straight. Mr. Leath's thought was to create an unusually stretchy yarn that could expand to fit various sizes and thus reduce the retail space required to display such a variety of stocking sizes. At the time, each pair of stockings was very specific in size to foot and leg. A woman who wore a size six shoe bought stockings knitted specifically for her length of foot.

Based on Mr. Leath's thoughts of creating a twisted 15 denier yarn, Mr. Bobo set about experimenting with various knitting techniques. After a few failures, he discovered that he could produce the stretchy yarn by incorporating a strand of silk. In 1955, the Leath-Bobo patent was issued, and a new era of perfectly fitting hosiery was born. By 1957, Mr. Leath and Mr. Bobo had taken the process one step further and given women their first taste of freedom by using their invention to produce the first generation of pantyhose. No more girdles or garters. My friend, unbeknownst to me for a long time, had been the coinventor of pantyhose. When he died, it was discovered that he held seven other patents, which, modestly, he had not divulged to even his closest friends.

Decades later, when a big dreamer by the name of Sara Blakely sought to manufacture her idea, she reached out to Mr. Bobo for advice to locate the knitting plants and resources she needed. Therefore, the man who was key in bringing pantyhose to the marketplace became key, almost fifty years later, in bringing the next most revolutionary product to women—Spanx.

Can you imagine how much more I learned from Mr. Bobo? His wisdom and life's experiments taught me, making me a better person, leading me to realize that an ordinary person can make extraordinary contributions. We each have that power. If only we choose to use it and live every day fully and with purpose. The day that Mr. Bobo took that phone call from Mr. Leath was just another business day. When he assembled his business team and began to devise a new technique, it was just another doing-business-as-usual day. Yet the everyday lives of generations of women were changed. Hundreds of millions of women across the globe over a span of time have felt more comfortable in their daily dressing habits because two men with strong work ethics were determined to give their best for a dollar's wage. Deep in the annals of history, if you search enough, you will find their names and contributions but their invention did not win them the fame afforded to Alexander Graham Bell, Jonas Salk, or Louis Pasteur. Still, it was important to the revolution of manufacturing and to the comfort of women.

Granted not all who grow old in years have wisdom because an ability to learn from experiences and formulate that into words and thoughts is as much a gift as the talent of playing the piano or sketching. To find a man or woman filled with astute wisdom is a remarkable treasure. All, though, have memories and recall times when photographs were developed in a dark room, phone booths existed with rotary dial phones, and clothespins were used to hang laundry on lines to dry in the warm sun and fresh air. When you listen to their stories, it's a living, breathing audio recollection of history and, too, they can always recall their own experiences of finding better days after trials and tribulations.

There's so much to be learned from those who have gone before us in this journey of life. It's about learning history, up close and personal with the added benefit of making those dear older people feel special and cherished. As the saying goes: It is a win-win all the way around and provides a wonderful opportunity to give back while taking in a meaningful way.

CHAPTER 20:

Focus on the Possibilities and Ignore the Improbabilities

O
ne of the big obstacles toward achieving improbable results in today's world is that there are too many facts put out there and those facts are too easily found.

You might be sitting in the airport, waiting for your flight to leave and pondering some "wild-eyed" idea you have.

"I wonder if anyone has ever done that?" You ask yourself. Then, you pick up your Smartphone, access the Internet, and discover that not only has it never been done, the odds are one billion to one that it can't be done. Poof. The pin of cold, hard facts burst your bubble, so you move on to something else.

Too much information has killed many dreams. Sometimes you have to purposely blind yourself to statistics and information so that you aren't overwhelmed by the improbability. It is best not to know what the world considers too hard or impossible to achieve.

When a friend was diagnosed with a terminal illness, another friend called me and said, "Get online and read everything you can about this cancer. Find out what we're dealing with." After all, that is what the majority of people do these days.

"No," I replied firmly. "I am not doing that. Facts can and will work against faith, if we let them. We have to believe with a pure innocence that everything can be all right. If this is as serious as the doctors say, then the facts will only undermine hope."

It is a theory to be practiced in all situations.

When I was a young girl in college and majoring in journalism and broadcasting, I got part-time jobs at a radio station and a daily newspaper. Education is wonderful, but nothing takes the place of on-the-job training where you'll truly learn the business. Since I was part-time with no experience, I found myself answering the phone and running errands. At the radio station, I was eventually allowed to write copy for commercials and unimportant news stories.

At the newspapers, I wrote obituaries from a one-page fact sheet that the funeral home directors brought in. It was no more than taking those facts and putting them into a readable form. I longed to do more. I studied the news room, looking deep for opportunities. A "wild-eyed" idea came to me, and since there was no way back then to easily research its viability, I became convinced that I could do that. I was the only one who thought so.

"I'm going to take up sports writing," I announced to the managing editor one day. In those days, women simply did not have that option open to them. Sports belonged to men and they were not giving up their turf or places in the press box.

The managing editor, a kindly, gentle soul, did not mock me. But he did not encourage me, either. I stood firm. Finally, he sighed. "Well, you'll have to talk to Jackson about that," referring to the sports editor.

The sports editor was typical of his generation—crusty, manly, cynical. I suspected he was also chauvinistic, though he would later disprove that. But he was very intimidating—so I approached him with fear and dread.

He laughed.

Did I mention that I knew NOTHING about sports? In the years hence, people have often asked me, "Were you a sports fan? Is that why you wanted to be a sports writer?"

Nope. Other than high school games, which I attended from a purely social aspect, I had never watched a game of any kind. Nor did I have the desire to watch one. At nineteen years old, though, I had an incredible instinct, one that even I didn't understand. I sensed that sports reporting offered an enormous opportunity for women. It was, no pun intended, an open field.

"You have to *know* about sports before you can *report* on them," he responded. He was absolutely right. For the next six months, I read sports-related books, *Sports Illustrated*, and three different sport sections daily. Helped by the kind of memory required for sports writing (one that retains statistics, numbers, and trivia), I took my newly invented self over to the weekly newspaper across town and convinced the editors to give me a chance. They were cynical, too, but they were desperate for reporters, so the editor gave me a shot. He paid me ten cents per printed inch for every article he used (ridiculous pay even then), but I gladly took it. I dug my high heels in and earned my chops. The first step in making the impossible into possible is to be willing to do whatever it takes to get a foot in the door. There has been a trend for the past decade or two for college graduates to actually believe—and some of this is encouraged by parents—that a certain high-level salary is owed because of a degree. Many refuse to do internships unless they're paid. As a novice, I did work for free or little money, just to get the experience. I was thrilled to get it. Each piece of nonpaid work was a stepping stone to eventually being well paid and turning fantasies into a reality.

A year later, the cynical sports editor called and offered me a job. "I can only pay you eight dollars an hour plus expenses," he said, shaking his head as if he were ashamed of the low pay. I was overjoyed. I was still in college, but very soon I was writing stories that were being picked up by national news services. In more than one instance, I became the first woman to cover this or that sports event, and in the beginning, I would always be the only woman in the press box. I won awards, too, becoming the first woman to pick up some sports writing awards.

Had I known more than I knew then, I would have surely been put off by the facts and statistics. I would have been blinded to great possibilities because of what the world considered "improbable." Among many valuable lessons I learned from that situation also came this: from that moment forward, I have believed passionately that *anything* is possible as long as you believe and work hard.

If you're unhappy with a job or career path, reinvent

yourself. It's only too late when you're six feet under. My friend, Judi Turner, is an amazing example of someone who did just that. I was in college when I watched that determined woman make a career change that many thought impossible. Perhaps her story will inspire you. Judi had used her journalism degree wisely so that by her early thirties, she was situated in a solid public relations job. She earned extra money by taking freelance assignments for newspapers and magazines. A child who had grown up on beach music and rock and roll, she discovered an affinity for country music when she took a freelance gig to interview the Oak Ridge Boys, a superstar group of the eighties.

It was like she had been born again—almost in the evangelical sense of the word. She wasn't only passionate about entertainment journalism, she was obsessed as it pertained to country music. Very quickly her college PR job became boring and unfulfilling. She pitched ideas to the local daily newspapers, and when they couldn't pay, she wrote for free. She began making friendships and connections. She made up her mind: She was going to move to Nashville and work in the music industry. Nothing would stop her. She made regular five-hour drives to Nashville in search of work. Her uncle was an emergency room doctor at a Nashville hospital, so she often stayed with him. She worked fervently but made little headway. It's hard to work your way into a tight industry that doesn't throw out the red carpet for newcomers.

Judi would not be dissuaded. After a year, she managed to get an entry-level job as assistant to the director of the prestigious Country Music Association. The pay was almost starvation level, a pittance compared to what she had been earning. She didn't bat an eye. Instead, she was overjoyed for the opportunity. There she was, a woman who had been well-established as a career professional with good benefits and salary, starting over as an assistant. Judi knew, though, that it was only a starting point. Fairly quickly, she worked her way up in the most important organization in the music business, becoming director of public relations for years until she struck out on her own to open a public relations company that represented many major country music stars. She became a "name" in the business. She did whatever it took—hard work and starting over—to make her dream possible. Taking determined control of her future, she not only created a better day for herself, she made the *best days* of her life happen, as did another friend of mine.

Richard Paul Evans, known as Rick to his friends, became a publishing phenomenon through a sweet book he had written as a gift of love to his children. "Though I told them often of my love for them, I didn't believe they could understand it until they had children of their own," he explained. He wrote a book to explain and called it "The Christmas Box." He self-published twenty copies and shared them with family, who began to pass the book to others. Soon, demand grew, so Rick printed more copies.

Not only is Rick one of the nicest folks I ever met, he is smart. As an advertising executive, he knew a bit about marketing, so he set about the task of putting the book in bookstores in and around his hometown of Salt Lake City, Utah. As Rick points out now, "I was in advertising, so I had the means to self-publish. It became a function of trying to meet the demand." Still, he points out, "It was the book not the marketing, but the marketing was an essential part of its growth."

Word-of-mouth books, the ones that are built to lasting

success through a grassroots movement, are the dream of every author and publisher. Since Rick was both, he was living a double-sided dream. He grabbed hold of the rising tide and used his advertising savvy to full advantage over the following two years when, incredibly, this little self-published book out of Utah hit the *New York Times*'s best-seller list. When *The Christmas Box* hit number one on the list, it made history becoming the first self-published book to do so. A morning show appearance by the articulate, good-looking young father quickly garnered the attention of the New York publishing world.

"It was crazy," he said. "People started calling and making offers." In publishing, a badge of honor for a book is an auction in which two or more publishers bid for the right to publish. Nine publishers tossed their bids in over a two-day auction, with Simon and Schuster winning the rights at a then record amount of $4.2 million. Suddenly, a father's love story for his daughters, self-published quietly, was the talk of the publishing industry. At one point, the book, printed in both hardcover and paperback, was number one simultaneously on the *NYT* in both categories. The little book that was originally printed with just twenty copies has sold over eight million copies worldwide. What was considered to be impossible became a history-making reality. Impossible doesn't mean it can't be done, it only means it hasn't, so far, been done.

"I've always dreamed big," he admitted. "I'm just wired that way, but the success (of *The Christmas Box*), opened the door for even bigger dreams and made it easier for those around me to believe in me."

Naïveté can be an incredible asset when turning impossibilities into probabilities. My close friend, Stevie Waltrip, made history in the 1970s when she became the first woman to be allowed on pit road, where racecars are serviced, during a NASCAR race. There was a strict policy against it with the organization going far enough as to proclaim on pit passes "No Women Permitted in Pits." Stevie, though, needed to score (keep fuel calculation) for her husband, Darrell. Stubborn as her hair is red, she persisted until she was allowed in to work. "I wasn't trying to break any barriers or make a statement," she explains. "My husband needed me and I was determined I was going to help him in any way possible. It's as simple as that." As Darrell said when he was inducted into the sport's prestigious Hall of Fame, "If there was a Hall of Fame for women, my wife would be the first one inducted." Stevie, ignoring facts, broke through and blazed the trail for hundreds of women to follow after her.

So turn a deaf ear to naysayers and a blind eye to what the world touts as facts. It is a gift to be blinded to what the world says is improbable—it allows you to see clearly a world of possibilities.

CHAPTER 21:

It Only Takes One Yes to Wipe Out a Thousand No's

I n Nashville, Tennessee, there is no one in the music business more respected than Don Light. Now in his seventies, Don started out as a drummer on the Grand Ole Opry, but his shrewd business mind and wily instincts soon took him into the business side of music where he ran *Billboard* magazine and cofounded the Gospel Music Association and Nashville's first gospel music booking agency before settling into the management side of the business. He is both a legend and a library of information, having been eyewitness to and often a participant in the town's music history.

For three decades, I have been an eager student, riveted by his experience and sitting with him often to listen in rapt interest to fascinating tales. He has blessed my life with wisdom and instruction. I admire that no matter how strong the argument is on why one of his ideas won't work, he always has a stronger argument why it will. One of his earliest successes required endless arguments and a downright stubbornness not to take no for an answer.

Bill Williams, editor of *Billboard*, and part-time television weatherman, called Don sometime around 1970 and asked him to listen to the music of a young staff writer. Williams thought that Don might be interested in booking the young man for gigs.

"Back in those days, there were venues known as listening rooms and I had gained a bit of a reputation for being able to book them," Don explained. "I listened to his songs and I liked him. He was different."

That was the beginning of a relationship that would secure Don Light's reputation as a man with a sharp eye for talent as well as underscore his tenacity. Without Don's moxie and refusal to accept rejection, the world might never have discovered the incomparable Jimmy Buffett.

Don started booking him. "I'd get him in the places, but he'd get himself back. With Jimmy, it was easy repeat business because his ability to connect with the people who buy tickets is incredible."

He then started shopping him for a record deal with the understanding that if he got him a deal, he'd be his manager. But Nashville record executives weren't buying (though RCA's Chet Atkins enjoyed Buffett's unique sound), and even, according to Don, Nashville outsiders and renowned music men like Clive Davis and Phil Walden passed. Buffett, though talented, simply did not fit into any familiar category, and all feared that they couldn't get radio play for him, a necessity for selling records.

"Every label in town turned us down, most turned us down twice and a few turned us down three times. But we kept going back." This kind of persistence is standard for Don, who is undaunted by challenges.

"You never thought of giving up on him?" I asked him once when visiting in his office on Music Row.

He shook his head crowned in silver, took a slug of cold water then continued. "Never occurred to me. It would take us about six months to make the round of record labels, then we'd start over. Label executives turn over so much that I figured by the time we got back around to that label again, there'd be a new decision maker in place. I knew that if we kept going that sooner or later someone would give us a shot. They couldn't all be that dumb."

It took two years and at least two dozen rejections before Don Gant, a recently hired executive at ABC Records' new Nashville division, signed Buffett. The good news had barely registered when Gant begin second-guessing his decision. At a record company meeting in Los Angeles, he played some of Buffett's music and was rebuffed. His colleagues thought that Buffett, again so unique that he did not fit in any established category, would be a hard sell to radio. Gant, worried about the lack of support, returned to Nashville and offered to release Buffett from his contract so that he could find a more enthusiastic label.

"I told him, 'No way,'" Don Light remembered. "I figured if nothing else we'd at least have studio quality demos that we could use to pitch elsewhere."

Buffett had a moderate hit with a smooth ballad called "Come Monday." While the record label executives proved right in Buffett being a hard sale to radio, they proved wrong about something else—Buffett *could* sell records and plenty of them without airplay. From the beginning, his fan base was a grassroots, word-of-mouth phenomenon. What Don had spotted about Buffett was undeniably true—he had an onstage persona and connection with the audience that was unrivaled and those people bought his records without the encouragement of radio.

"I remember him playing Willie Nelson's festival and he went out to play—he had probably recorded three albums by then—and the audience sang along with every song," Don recalled. "It was remarkable. He wasn't getting airplay, so they weren't hearing the songs on the radio—they were buying the records." Yes, they were. One early album, void of radio promotion, had sold a quarter of a million copies at a time when well-promoted Nashville records sold only tens of thousands.

Buffett, the son of a Mobile shipyard engineer and grandson of a sea captain, had yet to find the nautical, tropical theme that would become his trademark, but he was inching close. Don flew to Los Angeles to meet Buffett for a show.

"I checked in and was going to my room when I met Jimmy in the hall with his guitar. 'Listen to what I just wrote,' he said. He came to my room and played it."

When the song ended, Don commented dryly, "Not bad," a remark he often uses after hearing a great song. "I knew it was a good song because there's not a bad word in that song."

At that night's show at the Roxy on Sunset, Buffett returned for an encore without the band and played his latest composition. The crowd's reaction promised that "Margaritaville" was headed toward stardom. No one knew then, though, that it would become an iconic song for a generation.

Early in his career, Don Light learned a valuable lesson that would stick with him: Every rejection is just one person's opinion. What one person might hate, another may be destined to love. You just have to keep going until you find the right person to say yes. Buffett was so unique that no one could figure out where he belonged or rationalize how he could sell records. Even today, he defies being pigeon-holed into a category. In fact, he *is* a category, one in which he solely resides and one that is astronomically successful. What many experts thought worked against him, actually worked for him in a way that is incomparable.

The beauty in lessons like this is the education it provides for future situations. Years later, Don was in another position of rejection with a new artist who was turned down by RCA Records, the label that Don believed needed the traditional-sounding singer at a time when Nashville's music was more polished and pop.

"I called RCA back and said, 'I'm not going to let you pass on him. You need him.'" With logic, he won and Keith Whitley, still considered one of the genre's greatest voices, responded by recording smash records and platinum albums. Sadly, he died young of alcohol poisoning after years of struggling with the bottle.

Take rejection lightly, never to heart, then walk next door to another person because the bottom line is this: You don't want to be with anyone, either personally or professionally, who doesn't believe in you or isn't enthusiastic about you. It will drag you down and keep you from success. Synergy is created when two similar forces come together and produce enviable results. Everyone has an opinion. Sometimes they will agree with you, other times, they won't. Shrug it off and keep going. Chalk up the no's and keep going. One yes has much more power than a thousand no's. Its power is so great that it can wipe out the memory of those rejections. When you get the yes you want, the no's will no longer matter.

"The lesson to be taken in the Buffett situation is not to accept no as an answer," Don said. "Keep going. Sooner or later, maybe it won't be a no. It just takes one chance. If you're talented enough and do it long enough, it'll work out."

CHAPTER 22:

Everyone Deserves a Second Chance because You Never Know When It Will Change a Life

Folks were pretty tired of Eugene Palmer and his ways. At forty-six, he had spent thirty years stirring up trouble and aggravation for most who knew him and certainly for those who loved him. His was a wild, restless spirit that grew furious and raged when mixed with pure white moonshine though in a normal state, he was kind and well liked. That restless spirit became completely uncontrollable when drugs were tossed into the mix.

"People were tired of the way I'd been livin'," he admits. "And I can't blame 'em." He dropped his head full of strawberry blond–colored hair now frosted generously with gray. "Ain't no amount of tellin' can show how ashamed I am of the way I lived. It was terrible."

As far as anyone can figure, Gene's serious problems began at eighteen when his brother, who had been out drinking with him one night, was killed in a car wreck while driving impaired. "I blamed myself somethin' terrible over that. I started drinkin' half a gallon of white whiskey a day, just tryin' to forget."

In the cemetery of a nearby country church, the entire front row of gravestones belongs to the Palmer family. One by one they dropped, most dying young. His daddy was "runned over" by a car; two brothers killed in car wrecks; two other brothers killed themselves with guns; one brother beat to death with a baseball bat; a brother-in-law electrocuted while working for a power company; his wife, Gene's sister, then drank herself to death; and another sister died of disease. Later, his youngest daughter was killed in a car accident. For Gene, it has been an endless stream of tear-soaked parades to that graveyard, causing sorrow to cling to his heart like a permanent tattoo. You have to know things like this to get anywhere close to understanding what turns a man mean. Few are born mean. Life and its hardships make 'em that way.

"Them's all my people there," he said on the day we first met at that small church. He pointed to the graves. I was there to do a speaking engagement, and when I arrived and stepped out of the car, four people piled out of a nearby vehicle.

"This is the day I've been dreamin' of." The voice of the

man somewhere in his late sixties was soft. He introduced himself, offered his hand, then named off his wife, daughter, and granddaughter. He went on to explain that he had been a longtime fan of my newspaper column and always wanted to meet me. He held up my latest book. "I just got it last night. I can't wait to read it." We chatted and he asked for a photo.

"You've got a lot of fans in prison. I got a lot of 'em to readin' you when I was in there." I smiled and though I was tempted to ask more about his incarceration, I refrained.

"I'm a preacher now," he said. "A lot of folks wouldn't believe that, knowin' how I used to live but I am. I'm a changed man. I'm startin' a prison ministry. I wanna help others find the hope that I have now." He tilted his head and studied me for a second. "You wouldn't believe the life I've had. I ain't proud of it, either. I'd be ashamed for you to know it all. I shore would."

Later, my brother-in-law, Rodney, who had known Gene since childhood, asked, "Did he tell you what he went to prison for?" I shook my head. "Murder. And it was brutal. Killed his girlfriend."

Since that introduction, I have come to know Gene Palmer as a gentle, sincere, God-fearing man who is humbled from his failings and deeply regretful for the harm and hurt he has caused. "I live with it every day," his said, his eyes filling with tears. "I can't ever escape all I've done. And I don't deserve to." Those like Rodney who knew him when he was whipping up trouble on a regular basis are awed by the change in a former troublemaker who now reaches out to help others like his old self.

"It goes to show," Rodney said, "that a man can change if you give him a chance."

It took forty-six years, though, for Eugene Palmer, known in prison as one of the meanest inmates ever, to make his change. His complete transformation, though, offers hope to the mothers, fathers, wives, husbands, and others who have a family member addicted to drugs, alcohol, and a life of crime. People can change. It's never too late. It is possible to find better days in the midst of hopelessness. If you have an addict or wayward, trouble-making soul in your life, you are well familiar with the string of upsets and setbacks that often come. You may have thrown up your hands and quit or you may want to but let this story of redemption undergird your heart with hope. It is always possible for a person to have an epiphany so powerful that change will draw him in. You have only to look at Gene Palmer to know that it can happen.

The first time he went to prison in 1958 was for a series of thefts. After a few years in prison, he escaped, was recaptured, and forced to serve his entire fifteen-year sentence plus five years for stealing a truck during the breakout. Twenty years in prison didn't change him. He was still mean when he got out, perhaps even meaner, because an animal that is caged and beaten repeatedly doesn't settle down a bit. The anger and resentment only builds and rages stronger.

"I stayed drunk when I got out," he admitted when I visited to learn more of his story. "Then I started doin' drugs, mixin' it in. I did crank. The minute I got out of prison I bought whiskey and was drunk by the time I got home." He started selling drugs. He stopped and dropped his head. "I ain't proud of it. Lord, I hate the way I lived and how I treated my family." His wife, mother, children, and others, though, stood firmly by him.

"I loved him," his wife, Lovena, explained. "I always believed in him." She stopped and pulled back a bit. "Now I cussed him a lot and I'd get so mad that I couldn't stand it but I never gave up on him."

Gene gazed at her with a look of quiet disbelief, one, albeit, filled with gratitude. A woman—be it a mother or wife—who stands steadfastly by a wayward man can use that love to change the hardest of hearts. But don't get the impression that it was easy for her. After all, Gene, at his no-good worse, took up with one of her sisters and then another. It was that last one—Birdell—where the real trouble happened.

"We'd get to drinkin' and doin' drugs and we'd try to kill each other," Gene said about Birdell. "The law got called on us once or twice and the sheriff chewed us out."

One night, they drank even more than usual and dropped acid with the whiskey. Gene woke up in jail three days later and asked, "Why am I here?"

"Because you killed her."

He has no memory of what the sheriff called the "most brutal execution murder I have ever seen. It was sadistic." In 1983, though, it was mostly circumstantial evidence. There was no gun powder residue on his hands and no blood on his clothes. Gene could not offer an explanation or an alibi, his memory wiped empty then and now by the drugs and drink. He was picked up a few miles away from the crime scene. The district attorney announced that he would seek the death penalty. A jury was selected but three days into the procedure, the DA offered Gene a deal, "Plead guilty and we'll give you life rather than send you to the electric chair."

Gene thought of his ailing mother who had suffered a recent heart attack and the agony he had already put his wife and children through. "I couldn't do it to my mama or them. Couldn't make them go through a trial so I took the deal. My attorneys begged me not to. They told me they could get me off." He falls quiet for a moment. "But I figured I belonged in jail. I wasn't no good for nobody."

He was sentenced to natural life plus twenty years consecutive plus one year consecutive. Gene stoically took the sentence, believing he had earned the sentence of dying in prison. He disliked himself as much as anyone else could dislike him. In prison, Gene, now completely embittered, was more than a handful of trouble. "Everybody there hated me," he said. "I was the devil."

Twenty-four years into his sentence, Gene began to attend a worship service by an outside group. "One night at 3 a.m. in my cell, I went down on my knees and I prayed. I felt the change in my heart that came about from that prayer." Others saw it, too. Gene, who had been anything but cordial or easygoing in the forty-four years he had spent behind cell doors, became a model prisoner. He was baptized in a mop bucket in the courtyard of the prison. There was no question in anyone's mind that the change was genuine.

"He straightened up. He changed in a way I didn't think was possible," Lovena said.

He began to pray regularly and became devoted to his Bible. If there was no hope for better days in this life, he believed there was hope after death. He accepted his fate and never considered the possibility of parole. That wasn't the deal he had made. But in January, two years after his conversion by faith, a prison official informed him that he was going home.

"That can't be," Gene protested. "There must be some mistake. I ain't suppose to ever get out."

She shrugged her shoulders. "We don't understand, but we've received papers to release you."

"It," he said with a steady look, "was a miracle. No doubt

about it."

When he was released, all the prisoners serving lifetime sentences—lifers—lined up to wish him well. "They said, 'We're here because we got hope today.' They believed that if someone as sorry as me could make a change and find a new life, they could, too. When you're sentenced to life, you stop believing in better days. Everything seems hopeless. Things can change, though."

Since his release a few years ago, Eugene Palmer has become a preacher, taking his testimony to churches and back to prison to remind folks that hope abounds even in the worst people and situations. "My daddy prayed many a prayer for me," he said. "And they finally worked."

He now battles leukemia. "Whether I get to stay here or go to heaven, it's fine with me."

On that spring day when first we met, he had said, "The Lord called me to preach, and I'm gonna help men like me who need to get their lives straight. Some of the men in prison, they ain't got nobody."

My life has been positively touched by Eugene because I am amazed by a man, once hard and hunted, who has such love and compassion in his eyes. His touch is now gentle, his words are spoken with kindness and even the law officers who arrested him now consider him a friend. What if he had been convicted then executed and not given a reprieve? A second chance changed not only his life, but the lives of others who have been inspired, encouraged, and taught by him. From his mistakes, he gained wisdom, the kind that is received well by others because they see the trace of sorrow that boldly outlines his words of advice.

There is no undoing the past. Eugene, with great sadness,

will tell you that. There is no forgetting or letting go of regret. Whether he is eating, sleeping, or combing his hair, the remorse like the smell of sour milk hangs in the air around him. Eugene, though, will tell you he's a better man now because of all he's been through.

A second chance is always worth giving—in his case, it was more than two—even if few seize the opportunity and make the most of it. It's worth it for the ones like Eugene who know what to do with one more golden shot at life. Everyone, who earnestly seeks to right the wrongs of his past, should be blessed with the opportunity to prove that people can change. We owe it to ourselves, if not to them.

"These years since I got out of prison have been the best years of my life," he said, his eyes again filling with tears. "I thought I didn't have no better days left when I was in prison but I was wrong. The best days of my life were still to come."

CHAPTER 23:

Some Things in Life Are Hard because They're Not Meant to Be. Other Things Are Even Harder because They *Are* Meant to Be.

O ne of my girlfriends was working her way through the normal ups and downs that come with any romantic relationship. During a particularly hard stretch, she was close to giving up.

"Why is this so hard?" she asked one night, her voice quivering. "If this were really meant to be, why is it so hard?"

It is one of the great mysteries of life. Why are some things so hard? Why, if some things are meant to be, are they so hard to make happen? The answer is simple yet complex. "Because," I replied, "sometimes it just is."

People give up on situations and relationships sometimes when they become extremely difficult because analytical reasoning would lead us to conclude, "Things that are meant to be are never this hard." We feel we are trying to force a round peg into a square hole. It's easier to walk away than push through. While sometimes we do need to walk away—in the case of physical or emotional abuse—other times, fate is just trying us to see how much we want something wonderful, to determine if we'll push through a mountain of adversity to obtain a great prize. There are times when things are hard because the sweetest reward lies on the other side of tremendous difficulty.

Conventional wisdom will always whisper, "If this were really meant to be, it wouldn't be so hard." And that is easy to believe, much easier than working through the difficulties of a situation. That one piece of human reasoning leads too many people to give up on a situation that would have enormous payoff, if only they stayed the course.

I think back to a story told to me by my friend and mentor, Richard Childress, who is known as one of NASCAR's greatest team owners. A ninth-grade dropout, Childress never had life easy. He basically just scrimped by in life, but he always had a lot of fun doing it. In the late 1960s throughout the 1970s, he was an independent racecar driver on the NASCAR circuit, meaning that he got no factory support from Detroit, making it hard to compete against drivers like Richard Petty, who was bolstered by auto manufacturers and big sponsors. Still, he enjoyed it and was wise with what little money he made, putting a down payment on a plot of land on which he built a shop.

In 1981, reigning NASCAR champ Dale Earnhardt had a falling out with his car owner. It was the middle of the season and Earnhardt had nowhere to go, but he had a decent sponsorship with Wrangler Jeans. Childress's hero, former racer and by then a successful car owner, Junior Johnson, sat Childress down for a serious talk.

"Get out of the car as a driver, put the kid in, and take the sponsorship," Johnson said. "You can make a good living as a car owner, but you're barely making it as a racer."

"It was the hardest decision I ever made," Childress told me. "I knew that if I got out of the car, I had to stay out. I didn't know if I could do it."

But he did and it turned out to be the best decision that he ever made. Earnhardt finished out the season with Childress but then left when the car owner insisted.

"I told him to go with a well-established team and let me get everything going and he could come back," Childress said. In 1984, after two years of driving for a respected team owner, Bud Moore, Earnhardt rejoined Richard Childress Racing as the driver of the number three car. In 1985, the Earnhardt/ Childress team hit a brick wall. Though they had won four races, it paled in comparison to the nine races that they had not finished because of engine failure. During that time, they were considered, at best, a mid-level team, capable mostly of winning when top cars fell out. There was a serious problem in the engine department at RCR and Childress, despite sleepless nights and much mental anguish could not pinpoint it and, therefore, could not solve it.

"Take me back to 1985," I said one day. "Do you remember

the frustration then?"

"Boy, do I. That was a rough 'un. The toughest part was knowin' that I had people dependin' on me and that I had to figure it out."

Halfway through the season, eighteen months before his contract expired, Childress offered Earnhardt his release. Things had become so hard that it didn't look like it was meant to be. The last thing he wanted on earth was to release the driver whom he felt was, hands down, the best, most determined driver in the field. Childress, though, felt it was the only honorable resort because a great driver can't win with equipment that breaks constantly.

"You're a champion and you deserve better equipment than we're giving you. I'm going to release you from your contract so you can find a better team."

They were sitting in the front yard of Childress's home near Winston-Salem, North Carolina. Earnhardt took a sip from the beer he was drinking and swallowed before answering. He locked his jaw in that stubborn way, familiar to all who knew him well. "No," he said in a voice that dared to be defied. "We started this thing together, and we'll finish it together."

"I'll never forget him saying that," Childress recalls. They were words that would build a bridge between ordinary and extraordinary.

Sixteen months after that conversation, the duo, who refused to give up when things got so hard, won the first of six national championships, making history along the way. Together, Childress and Earnhardt would become folk legends and rewrite the history of racing.

"We knew we had the right combination," Childress said. "So we just had to weather the storm. You can't just sit back and wait for the storm to pass, you have to work in the rain."

Richard Childress and Dale Earnhardt, who would "finish it together" on a February day during the Daytona 500 when Earnhardt was killed in a crash, won almost $40 million together and were bringing in $20 million annually in souvenir sales when death did part them. In their way, they answered that question: If something is meant to be, why would it be so hard? Because sometimes it just is. But the bigger the struggles, the greater the payoff. Had they not pushed through, most likely neither man would have found individually the success and rewards that they found together. At a point when it looked like there was nothing much left to do but quit—because it was too hard to figure out—they regrouped, took a deep breath, and burst through the wall of adversity.

Yes, sometimes it's hard because it isn't meant to be. How do you tell the difference? Through plain, common sense reasoning as well as instinct. Are you in a relationship where you're abused emotionally or physically? Are you in a job where your boss is dishonest? Is there anything about the situation that you're battling that doesn't make sense for you to continue?

If you're in a job where a coworker is making you miserable, but it's a good company with benefits and an opportunity to advance, push through. I once worked in a company with a whining complainer who caused problems for everyone. There were constantly little battles going on and, surprise, she was always the common denominator. The shame of the matter is that the young woman was smart and capable but she was also very insecure. She advanced by stepping on whomever she could. We hung in there, though, and one day she moved on to another job. She disappeared completely—no one has any idea where she is—while the others in the office went on to have successful careers.

If you're chasing a dream and keep running into dead ends, reassess your methods. Is there something you could do differently? Do you have a Plan B and a Plan C? Sometimes dreams run into trouble when you put too much pressure on them, especially financial pressure. If you have a dream of being an artist, entertainer, dancer, musician, writer, don't give up your job at a department store. You still need to make a living while you're chasing that dream.

Childress and Earnhardt instinctively believed they were the right combination. They knew that Childress was a shrewd businessman, skilled at running a team while Earnhardt had undeniable talent and courage as a driver. Together, they complimented each other's strengths and made a formidable partnership. The hard times they faced were just that—normal, everyday challenges though the obstacles looked insurmountable at the time. Because they didn't give up—even though they talked about it—they reached the mountain top of success.

The greatest happiness and successes are always preceded by challenges. It's the way we're tested to see how much we want something. If we don't want it that much, we'll give up. If we're really determined, we'll see it through. No matter how hard it is.

CHAPTER 24:

You Get What You Settle For

When I was touring with my first book, I appeared at a couple of trade shows and book festivals that allowed me the privilege of meeting two other first-time authors, both who became friends but, most importantly, who demonstrated that if we take charge, we don't have to settle for less than what we want. It was a remarkable lesson.

Dorothea Benton Frank, Dottie to her friends, is probably the most energetic, dynamic woman I have ever met. She is spectacular in every way. Jill Conner Browne is quiet, soft-spoken, and lovely. Both are driven, determined, and have a laser-like focus on any goal they set. Though their life stories and journeys are very different, one thing is remarkably similar: They both put down a foot and refused to take only whatever life dictated. They decided to manage their destinies. Neither was willing to settle for less than they wanted.

Dottie, who has a boundless amount of enthusiasm and drive, grew up on Sullivan's Island in South Carolina, a place she loved dearly. There is something about home to Southerners that runs deep in our hearts, and though Dottie eventually became a powerhouse in the apparel industry in New York and married well, she always had a longing for home. It called persistently to her. When her childhood home went up for sale, it was of paramount importance for her to own it. She begged her husband to buy the house, but he steadfastly refused.

"He could have bought it with his pocket change that had fallen into the sofa, but he wouldn't do it," she explained in a library event we did together. "So, I made up my mind that I would do it."

Incredibly, she just up and decided that she would write a book, sell it, and use the proceeds to buy the Sullivan's Island home. Dottie is one of the few people—maybe the only person—who would ever seriously consider that was actually possible. She had never written a book, first of all. Secondly, rarely does a first novel earn enough money to buy a set of dishes, let alone a whole house. Thirdly, she was a novice to the publishing industry. None of this stopped her. In fact, none of it probably even occurred to her.

She sat down, wrote a piece of Southern fiction about the place that held her heart and, fittingly, called it *Sullivan's Island*. Then, she guided it to an agent, a small auction, and a two-book deal.

Soon she set off in a media and marketing frenzy. She did

whatever it took to promote the book. The fact that she had, in her first effort, written a page-turner backed up all her efforts and gave her something fantastic to promote. The book gained traction from the moment it hit shelves, mainly by word-of-mouth. Within a month, it was obvious that Dottie had a runaway best seller.

During the first few weeks of its release, I was in Charlotte, North Carolina, to do a book signing at a well-known bookstore and the owner said, "We can't keep *Sullivan's Island* on the shelves. It sells at lightning speed and rightly so. It's thoroughly enjoyable." In the first few months, *Sullivan's Island* sold hundreds of thousands of copies and climbed effortlessly onto every best seller list in the nation. Now many books later, she is a fixture on the *New York Times* list. Dottie Benton Frank did not settle. When she saw what she wanted, she went for it and she got it. In fact, she didn't just get it in a plain, ordinary way, she got it big, in an explosive, history-making way.

Jill was a single mother who had spent too many years just scraping by. She worked as a fitness trainer, rising early in the morning, making breakfast and packing a lunch for her daughter, Bailey, then hurrying out the door before the sun had risen. Life hadn't been easy, but Jill never complained. She just dug in her heels and worked as hard as it took to pay the bills. She began writing a newspaper column on fitness using a natural gift for storytelling and an incomparable sense of humor. She's deceptively reserved but as funny as they come, and she seamlessly weaves Southern vernacular into her prose, holding her own among the best of Southern storytellers.

Someone suggested that she take her obvious talent and write a book about the exploits and wisdom of a group of friends with whom she had formed a sorority over a decade earlier to offer sisterly support, preach the empowerment of women, and have spirited fun. *The Sweet Potato Queens' Book of Love* inched its way toward a major bestseller by way of a grassroots movement, a word-of-mouth campaign where women who had read it heartily recommended it to others. For Jill, who used savvy, marketing smarts and good old-fashioned elbow grease (it was a lot more fun than getting up before dawn to work long hours as a personal trainer), it became a cottage industry loaded with other bestsellers, speaking engagements, and countless merchandising opportunities.

The night I met her, I sat down beside her at a private party at the Country Music Hall of Fame in Nashville and talked. Her book had been out for a few months and was starting to get a real buzz. "If I could just make enough money to take care of me and my daughter, I would be happy," she commented quietly. "If I could just make a million dollars."

That kind of money sounded like an out-of-the-orbit number to me but, lo and behold, she made it and much more. Her first book had been through many printings before she finally decided to get an agent, but that agent brilliantly negotiated a major seven figure deal for the next books, a contract that turned out to be a wise investment for the publisher.

I was having dinner one night with a childhood friend. Really, he had been my nemesis back in those days of youth. Typical boy-and-girl things where he played mean tricks and then I would chase him with a baseball bat but never come close to catching him. The childish things eventually passed away and by the time we were teenagers, we were pals.

We were well into our adult stages of learning lessons the night we dined and began a discussion about the folks we had both dated. He told me of a serious relationship he had in college, which happened to be someone I knew. I was astounded. I would never have pictured them together. She was cute in a plain way, and he was handsome. She was serious and sharply smart, and he wasn't either of those. He told me how he had broken up with her one night, in the gentlest way possible, but she was crushed. She thought they would marry.

"I have to hand it to her," he said. "She never called or tried to get back together. She was hurt, but she walked away with her head high. I respected that."

"Why did you break up with her?" I asked.

He looked me squarely in the eye for a long moment, the thoughts clearly running through his head. "Seriously?" he asked quietly.

I leaned closer. "Seriously."

"I've never told anyone this." He stared out the window for a moment, then turned back to me. "I thought I could do better."

It was the bravest statement I had ever heard. How many people think that but would never admit it? Neither to themselves or anyone else. But there's no sin in that. The sin is to settle for less than you want in life. So many people, particularly women, settle for less than what they want in a relationship. As a result, they never have true contentment, peace, or happiness. Before you marry someone, ask yourself: "Will I ever wonder if there's anyone better out there? Or is this the person who can completely satisfy my heart?"

People settle in many ways. A law enforcement friend says that many criminals are repeating a family pattern. They settle for life as they were born into it and do not try to escape it. In the deepest part of the Appalachians, there is often a family cycle of no advanced education (indeed, many drop out of high school rather than finish) and marrying young followed by children and a lifetime of barely scraping by. It is an endless cycle of hard lives. I had the opportunity to meet a pretty young woman in the mountains, who was exceptionally bright. She was hungry to learn and read books constantly, arising to read early in the morning, then reading herself to sleep at night. When she was sixteen, I offered her a chance to escape the cycle by coming down from the mountains to live with me while working a summer job. Her parents supported the idea because they realized that the cycle had to be broken. But she was too scared to leave the comfort of what was known for what was unknown. She could not be convinced against settling, so she turned it down. Just out of high school, she got pregnant and then again a short time later. Cycles have to be consciously broken.

Whatever you want—a spouse, job, particular college—set your standards high and don't settle. It's easy sometimes to take what you can see rather than holding out for what isn't visible, but the payoff for waiting is always worth it.

Like Dottie and Jill, if you're lacking something that you want, don't settle for life without it. Be brave and bold. Step out and start swinging your arms until you catch it.

CHAPTER 25:

Life Is Full of Wonderful. You Just Have to Remember to Look for It

I remember the July day covered with the kind of dust that comes when rain doesn't. It was when I visited a woman, old and gray, her journey of life nearing its winter's end. She settled into an armless rocker and moved gently, slowly back and fro, looking from her visitor to the books that scattered the rooms of the small, plain house that sat beneath the towering magnolia trees, spreading the full length of her yard.

"Oh, isn't life wonderful?" she asked, her sweet voice full of Southern accented exuberance and her faded blue eyes flickering with joy. Over ninety years of living had not dampened her enthusiasm nor had it slowed her down. "I've been blessed, so very blessed." She smoothed the cotton fabric of the top she wore and lightly touched the wrinkled cheek that had melted downward with age and hung in folds around her mouth.

She spoke with grand fondness for the years that had passed, the smile never fading from her still rosy lips. There was that handsome man, newly returned from a world war, who had breezed into her life and swept her away.

"Never did one woman love a man more," she said so convincingly that I knew it was truth, not a memory enhanced romantically by the time that had slipped by. "I loved him from the first date and he loved me, too. I married him three months later, and it was pure bliss. It was the ten happiest years of my life."

"Ten years?" I took a sip of the iced peach tea. It was instant tea that she had stirred up in the tiny kitchen as I leaned against the cabinet and watched. Outside the window over the sink, a bird lighted on the sill and flittered off quickly when its tiny feet touched scorching brick.

Her blue eyes suddenly fogged with the memory. "He died in my arms. It was sudden, unexpected." Her wistful sigh floated across the air and hit my heart with a thud.

I swallowed hard—love so strong and true yet gone so quickly. She had lived over sixty years past that blissful time of marital love.

"Did you ever come close to marrying again?" I wanted the story to have a happier ending. It is the undeniable romantic in me.

She smiled and shook her head. "Never crossed my mind. Once you've known such pure happiness with a man you love like I loved him, anything else would fall way short."

I found Kathryn Tucker Windham by accident or, perhaps, divine fate. I was in Williamsburg, Virginia, for a speaking engagement when I heard there was a storytelling event in town. I had long heard of those gatherings where renowned storytellers enthralled audiences with their skills. Though the tickets were sold out, a friend and I convinced the ticket takers to allow two more. We strolled in and stopped at the concessions tent where I asked the vendors to recommend the best storyteller.

"Miss Kathryn Tucker Windham," the lady said. "Ain't no competition. She's the best."

I bought two CDs and fell promptly in love with her gentle storytelling that is lyrical and reminiscent of times past, told in a sweet song of a Southern accent. Her stories aren't dramatic or loaded with bombshell endings. They are simple but intriguing, illustrating that compelling stories can be found in ordinary recollections and circumstances. On the day I had the pleasure of her company, her storytelling ways had earned a place of reverence in the realm of national public radio. When she kindly called to thank me personally for a column I had written about her, I jumped at the chance to make her acquaintance. That's how I wound up in her hometown of Selma, Alabama, that summer afternoon.

"Now, you're comin' to the poor side of town," she warned in her trademark, lilting drawl drifting over the phone line.

"Don't expect nothin' fancy."

Without trouble, I found my way to her little saltbox house where she had lived for the majority of her life. Throughout the sunny afternoon over glasses of tea, we continued our conversation and I listened to her tales of a blessed life. She had settled into life as a "widow woman" with three small children to raise and made her reputation as one of the South's most respected newspaper reporters. This was in the days when women were relegated to writing obituaries and covering afternoon teas and society weddings, but she had blazed trails by covering hard news. When the Civil Rights marches took over the front page in the 1960s, she was there in the trenches, praying that Martin Luther King Jr. could lead his people to victory.

"I knew every word of every song of the movement," she recalled. Her face clouded. "I never saw such hate as I saw in the faces of those who opposed it. I'll never forget the look of that kind of hate." She shuddered from the memory.

Repeatedly, she talked on and on about how blessed her life had been, then insisted on pulling out old photos, many of them black-and-white. She pointed out her children in varying ages, then her voice grew soft, wistful again.

"He died suddenly, young." She pointed to a handsome man in his thirties who had been her son-in-law, loved like a son by her. "Internal bleeding. They couldn't get it stopped." She picked up a photo of a middle-aged woman. "She was my oldest. Died a few years ago of a massive stroke." Gently, she set the photo back down. "Losing a child is the greatest sorrow you'll ever carry. It's terrible," she said, fluttering the pronunciation where such a sad word sounded almost pretty. "Just terrible."

The sadness was momentary. She stilled herself, pulled back her shoulders, and smiled beautifully. "Just look at how blessed I've been." She motioned at the photos. She put a frail hand on my shoulder and smiled genuinely. "Isn't life wonderful?"

She pulled books from the many scattered about that spilled through the room and offered them as gifts. A couple she had written but others were ones she had enjoyed and simply wanted to pass along the experience of joy.

"Did you see this?" she asked, motioning to a framed, handwritten note that hung on the wall next to my shoulder. I read the note silently, finished the last couple of sentences aloud, and looked over at her. I didn't recognize the name.

She beamed. "That's my dearest friend, Nell. We visit a great deal. I go to see her every chance I get. I like to keep her cheered up." She shared a couple of stories about their friendship.

Her dearest friend is known to the rest of the world as Harper Lee, Pulitzer Prize–winning author of *To Kill a Mockingbird*.

I drove out of Selma that afternoon, crossing the famous Edmund T. Pettus Bridge, the one marked in history by Dr. King and his people, but my mind stayed tucked back in the living room of Miss Kathryn's house. Life, it seemed, had been unkind and unfair. She had been widowed at a young age, a woman who had lost a great love after only ten years together and had raised three small children on her own. Then, the children had started dying. Yet, this woman who had never known extraordinary comfort or wealth in life, was determined to see the beauty in life. She not only found wonderful, she *made* wonderful. She took heartbreak and turned it into smiles. She began with her words, for she, the storyteller that she was, knew the power of words, both spoken and written.

"Isn't life wonderful?" she had said over and over that afternoon, a glorious smile gleaming from her eyes and lips. "I'm so blessed. So very blessed." She meant it. Instead of dwelling on the sorrows, she had found wonderful amidst the sadness.

I learned long ago that good rises up out of the bad. We have only to seek it by searching through the ruins to find it. Sometimes, though, it finds us. From the breakup of a relationship, we are led down a path that brings an encounter with a stronger, better love and companion. The loss of a job can force us to look around and pursue an avenue that leads us on a new adventure, one we wouldn't trade to have the other job back. Financial difficulties can teach us to avoid the same mistakes again and bring us to a prosperity we would not have had otherwise, without having learned the lessons of the missteps. If we stay focused on the bad, talk endlessly about it and cling to it the way a child hugs a blanket, we will never uncover the good, the gift delivered by way of the bad. It's such a waste of precious life to drag through day after day, pulled down by worries, regret or sorrow. There is joy to be found in every day, so when you wake up in the morning, center yourself on those blessings.

If you're having a hard time, make a list of several things that would be worse than anything you're going through. You'll be surprised at how quickly your attitude will straighten up. One day I was driving home from an appointment and was deeply troubled by something. I can't even recall what it was, but I was totally focused on the pain connected with it. I turned into my driveway, which is a long approach toward my house. Suddenly, I stopped the car. "Look at your blessings," I said to myself. I tear in and out of that driveway daily and barely notice the wonderful that surrounds me. For a long time I sat there and absorbed the beauty of the trees; the green pasture; the small river that winds through it; the bubbling stream that runs under the driveway and flows into the river; the cattle chewing grass quietly; my cat that scampered playfully; and my house and garden. I focused on every individual blessing and turned my thoughts from the silly trouble on my mind. I chastised myself for focusing on one small problem while being blind to an abundance of blessings.

Almost a year after our visit, Miss Kathryn, ninety-three, passed gently into eternity to be reunited, as the Sunday School teacher in her believed, with the loved ones who had passed on before her. She was placed in a handmade coffin she had long kept tucked away in the shed behind her house, put in a red pickup truck, and transported with little fanfare to the cemetery for a quiet burial that ended with the old gospel hymn, "I'll Fly Away." The accomplishment of her life as a storyteller, reporter, and historian earned a lengthy obituary in the *New York Times* and a farewell on National Public Radio.

I was one of many touched by her art, but I was privileged to be blessed by the philosophy of her experience: Life is truly wonderful. You just have to look for the wonderful. It's there.

CHAPTER 26:

You're Never Too Old to Find Your Dream

While in Dallas on a book tour, I ran into Paula Deen, also on a book tour, at a television morning show on which we were both appearing. Paula had been gracious enough to blurb the book that I was promoting, so she came over to ask how the book was doing. It was more than a courtesy. She was sincere. She took my hands, squeezed them tightly, looked straight into my eyes, completely focused and asked meaningful questions. Her own beautiful blue eyes were bloodshot, and I could detect weariness in her face. Grueling book tours are hard, especially for someone like Paula who will sign several hundred copies at each stop. She is a workhorse, though. She is so grateful for her blessings and opportunities that she will work as long and as hard as it takes.

And with good reason: She was firmly in middle age before she found her dream. I had already done my interview, but I stayed to watch her. That day, the television host, clearly smitten with the vivacious Paula, said, "Now, you were older when you found success, right?"

"Honey!" She rolled her eyes comically, enchantingly. "I was past fifty when I got my own television show, and then I fell in love and got married after that." She reached over from her place on the sofa toward him in the chair where he sat and laid her hand on his. "The best part of my life came after I passed fifty and, honey, I'm here to tell you that it's never too late to have everything you want in life. I'm livin' proof."

Paula scraped by for years, barely making a living, and striving to overcome personal struggles. She did, though, what every person who finds their dream has to do: She kept pushing forward. Despite the setbacks and the discouragements, she got up every morning, put one foot in front of the other, and just kept going. She found a way to make a living by employing her love of cooking when she set up a home-based catering business. As she grew older, she could have grown discouraged. She could have said, "This is the best it's ever going to be" and left it at that. But Paula delighted in every small triumph that came her way. She was grateful when the catering business grew to a restaurant in her hometown of Savannah. Then Oprah found her and invited Paula on her show. After a couple of guest appearances on the Food Network, Paula got her own show.

But getting the show that would make her a superstar wasn't a cinch.

She told me once, a few years ago, that the producer, Gordon Elliott, who had seen her on other food shows, believed in her so much that he took her to his agent for representation. He knew she needed her own show.

"For two years, Gordon and his agent shopped a show for me," she said. "And no one was interested. Everyone said that no one was interested in Southern cooking." She stopped and smiled. "Gordon refused to give up. He even built a kitchen in his own house in New York where we could shoot the show."

Television has a fixation with youth. Paula and Gordon could have been intimidated by that. After all, she was well into middle age by that point. Both refused to buy in to what some people believe: Dreams and success belong to the young and only they can grab the golden ring. It's probably fair to say that there has never been a bigger smash hit in the world of cooking than Miss Paula Deen of Savannah, Georgia. She has two hit television shows, turns up regularly on major network shows as a guest or host, has dominated the bestseller lists with her cookbooks, and is a licensing giant, having put her name on everything from cookware to restaurants to country hams. Whenever she appears on a shopping network, her products sell out in minutes. To me, though, her greatest success isn't fame, fortune, or even the goodwill and compassion that she pours out on those in need, it is the example that she has set by finding phenomenal success after the age of fifty. Her life is one that we should all emulate—get up in the morning, put one foot in front of the other, and keep believing that the best is yet to come.

Karen Peck, one of my best friends and a multiple Grammy Award–nominated singer, often says, "I haven't recorded my best song, and you haven't written your best book yet. The best still lies ahead for us." That's such an optimistic take on things because as Karen says, "We can't ever believe that the best is behind us. We have to believe it's still ahead."

The saddest thing I ever heard was a friend, now in his late sixties, who lamented about lost opportunities. He has had a good life, but it wasn't the one he dreamed of living. "My life doesn't look anything like I always thought it would." His eyes filled with tears. "I let too many things get away. It's too late to find those dreams now."

"No, it's not," I protested. "It's only too late when the last breath is gone."

He shook his head. "No, it's too late."

Now, at the age of sixty-five or seventy, it is too late to win the Heisman or Miss America—there are age limits on those, you know—but it's not too late for other dreams. Or to tweak the original dream. If you can't compete for the Heisman, then coach football. If you can't participate in the Miss America pageant, work with pageants in other ways. Yet, there are so many dreams that you can still chase and catch—writer, artist, singer, college graduate, business owner, hairdresser, marathon runner, world traveler, actor, teacher, preacher, horse trainer, concert pianist, and the list goes on and on.

I met a woman once who became a very successful print model when she was sixty. Since she was a little girl, she dreamed of being a model, but she got married young, had children, and just got too busy. When all the children were grown, she went to a modeling agency and found a lucrative niche modeling for products and services that targeted "youthful seniors." Had she simply accepted her dream was gone because of her age, she would have lost it forever. Sometimes, we simply have to reinvent dreams, and we have to envision them in a new way.

Nothing is sadder than folks who get to the age of forty-five, then throw up their hands and quit. Too many people believe that if you haven't made your dreams come true by the age of forty, then you've lost your chance. That's simply not true. Not all people are destined to have success early in life. In actuality, the dreams that come to fruition later in life are enjoyed more and appreciated on a deeper level because we realize how fortunate we are to have those. Youth often takes too much for granted. Tremendous success can be hard to manage because it can bring an arrogance that will trick us into letting up and eventually losing what we had.

Some people—like Paula—are destined to find it later in life. No doubt she would tell you that it was worth all the struggles to get to the place of joy that she has today. She will also tell you that the reason she works so hard and doesn't let an opportunity pass is because you have to make hay while the sun shines. In farmer's terms, once hay is cut if the rain hits it, it is ruined. Farmers hurry to cut the hay in a timely manner and gather it into the barns before rain comes. Those who become successful at an early age will often take opportunities for granted. Not when you're older, though. You know what it took to get there so you take advantage of every opportunity that comes.

What if Paula had given up? What if she bought into the "dreams are only for those of child-bearing years?" It would have been not only her loss but ours as well. She is truly a unique woman who sprinkles joy and laughter wherever she is. She is also a spokesperson for hope and a reminder that life can bring many wonderful things your way regardless of age.

You're never too old to find your dreams. Your best days are still to come. Isn't that a lovely thought?

CHAPTER 27:

You Learn More from Those Who Are Dying Than Those Who Are Living

Several years ago, a friend passed away. I had visited with him on his terrace shortly before death had plucked at his ear and summoned him. By accounts of earthly measurement, he was impeccably successful. His career had been stellar, and he had shared generously with those around him.

But as death eased with certainty toward him, he had regrets. Not the kind of minor regrets that we all have but the toxic large regrets that chew through a man's soul and leaves it riddled with holes.

"I've made a lot of money," he said with a shrug. "Now, I'm leaving it for the vultures to fight over. All that money can't heal my body or bring forth the peace of a satisfied man."

My eyes watered as I studied the regret and disappointment in his faded eyes. I knew he had spent years chasing success as a way of covering up for the personal happiness he neglected.

"What's your biggest regret?" I asked, believing he would tell me. In fact, I felt he needed to get it off his chest.

He swallowed hard and looked away, focusing on a hawk that coasted lazily through the blue sky. He sighed and I could hear the heartbreak in that deep breath. "I let the woman I loved get away. Pretended it didn't matter. That as long as I could make money, I could have anything I wanted on earth and be happy." He shook his head. "What a fool was I."

I wanted to cry but for his downtrodden sake, I didn't. He turned his eyes to me. "Now you listen to me: don't let that happen to you. Nothing's more important than love. No amount of money or success can equal it."

The words of a dying man are always the truest ever spoken. There is a clarity presented by the approach of inevitable demise that is unmatched in wisdom. Finally, the mind listens clearly to the heart, ignoring selfish will and societal pressures.

I have little doubt that no man or woman who ever chose money or profession over family and love, was happy with that choice in their latter years. An abundance of money and possessions cannot fill the void created by a lack of love. Over the years, I have seen many who pursued self over others throughout their lives and, inevitably, they wind up alone. Their greed melts into a human need for emotional involvement and compassion from others. However, the children they neglected while spending long hours at the office or the great love they turned aside in order to make another dollar, have followed the example set before them—they're either long gone or too busy to share even the briefest of phone conversation.

It is possible to have it all. But, first, one must be willing to give it all.

My childhood friend—the boy who had pulled my pigtails, mocked my freckles—was dying. Young, handsome, and still a bachelor, he was dying much too soon. But cancer does not discriminate. It can choose those dewy with youth, those healthy and stout, or those brittle with age. I had given up young friends to the grave before but this time was different. This was someone with whom I had a bounty of history, and while the others had died quickly and unexpectedly, he was inching slowly toward demise. He had time to tell me what the impending arrival of death had taught him.

One afternoon, I sat on the sofa beside his recliner, my knitting needles clicking furiously as we watched television. The movie finished, he clicked off the power and we began to talk. He was three weeks away from his final breath, but we didn't know that then. We still lived in a bubble of optimism that a miracle could happen and the disease could magically disappear. Correction: I lived in that bubble. He was more mature and braver than I. He was resigned to the prognosis, knowing that he had lived eighteen months longer than the original six weeks that the doctors had predicted.

"You know that song where the man is dying, so he goes out

and does all the things he never had time to do like bull riding and mountain climbing?" he asked. I nodded silently. "Well, when I found out I was sick, I didn't want to do any of those things. I just wanted to come home, bring all the people I love here and just look at them, spend time with them. That's all I wanted."

He smiled tiredly. "I used to get mad at this brother or that sister over something that seemed important. But when I got sick, each one of them has done everything possible to help me." He began to list the myriad kindnesses. When he finished, he sighed. "I wish I could take back any ugly words or arguments with my loved ones. They always loved me so much, but sometimes I refused to see it."

See, most of us get it wrong. We think that houses, cars, and jobs are more important than the ones around us who will be there when that job disappears with a downsizing and takes those houses, cars, and boats. Well, we don't really *think* that. We just *act* that way. We put a deadline assignment before a child's baseball game, a spouse's dinner party, or a family get-together. Not choices, surely, we would make if the end of life was just around the corner. Sometimes, because of a financial downturn or other struggle, we think we're in a bad time when, in reality, we're in a period that we will one day recall as "good days." The challenge is to see those good days and enjoy them rather than longing for them once they're gone.

Listen to those who are approaching the end of life, absorb their wisdom and use it—for they are in a place that you aren't and you don't want to be. They know what all of us should remember—material possessions are nice but nothing when compared to health and relationships with those dear to us.

When I decided to be a sports writer, I set out to learn the history of each sport and somewhere along the way became enthralled with former New York Yankees great, Mickey Mantle. Well over twenty years after his retirement from baseball, his charisma was still such that it reached out and grabbed a young girl. I became somewhat of a historian on the famed center fielder.

Though I never met him personally, I knew several who knew him quite well and all told stories of a troubled man. His drinking was legendary and, sadly, his alcoholism was shared by every member of his family, including his wife. A couple of years before his death, he sought treatment and overcame it, but his liver could not recover. After he sobered up, he looked back on his life with strong remorse. Though he was one of the most celebrated athletes in history, all he could see was regret for the partying, other women, and how he had neglected his family. "I wasn't a good dad," he said sadly.

When Mantle died, Grand Ole Opry member and former *Hee Haw* star Roy Clark, like Mantle an Oklahoma native, sang at his funeral, which was televised. The song he sang—"Yesterday When I Was Young"—is a mournful, heartbreaking ballad of regret for a life thrown away. I was astounded because it was such an odd selection for a last good-bye.

A few years later, I had the privilege of meeting Roy Clark after one of his shows. We struck up quite a conversation, connecting on various points of interests. After a while, I felt comfortable enough to ask him what I had long wondered.

"I'm a huge Mickey Mantle fan," I began.

He grinned. "Oh, great guy. He was such a good friend." He shook his head. "I miss him so much."

"I have to ask—why did you sing *that* song at his funeral? It haunts me."

A cloud of sadness covered the face of the legendary star. He dropped his eyes for a moment, shook his head, then looked back at me. "He insisted. He had told me years before that when he died, he wanted me to sing that song. I said, 'Oh no, Mickey. You don't want that song,'" Clark said. Mantle, though, could not be swayed. That was how he felt about his life. As far as he was concerned, it was the ugly truth, and he would not back down from accepting responsibility for it. When Mantle's health was crumbling, he called Clark and firmly reminded him of his promise to sing the song. And so he did.

As Mantle was dying, he took occasion to tell kids to use him as a role model of what not to do in life rather than how to live. It's a story that covers my heart in a residue of sadness. Mantle's accolades, awards, and astounding achievements made him one of the country's most famous men, yet at the end of his life, he could not see the good he had accomplished for the dark shadows cast over them by his mistakes and bad choices. Fame and fortune had been his, but peace of mind and satisfaction escaped his grasp.

We all need to take the time to listen closely to what impending death makes clear to others. If we do and we take those lessons to heart, we'll make better choices for our own lives.

CHAPTER 28:

It's Not What You Earn That Counts, It's What You Keep

I descend from many generations of frugal people, a nice way of saying "downright stingy." They spent their lives scraping together money for taxes and living off the land as much as possible. They, Appalachian people, were ingenious in finding ways to survive, a skill they passed down to their children and their children to their children. There was no sterling silver to pass along but an ability to manage a dollar has turned out to be more valuable.

When Nano was ninety years old, she had already had a full

lifetime of watching every penny. Her husband had died at an early age and had left her with babies to raise on her own during the days of the Great Depression when many areas of the Southern mountains were like a third world country. Nano hadn't had indoor plumbing (nor did any of her neighbors), so every day she had had to carry heavy buckets of water from a creek to her house. She had milked a cow for dairy, including butter, had counted on a scrawny chicken for eggs, had planted a summer garden, and had been a good enough of a shot to kill a wild hog from time to time for meat. Without a husband, the burden of taxes, medicine, and clothing had fallen solely on her back. It had been a grim, back-breaking existence, but she had made it through and had lived to tell about it. When she was old and bent over from the burdens and heavy work, she would say from time to time that those years had almost killed her and, if it hadn't been for her children, there would have been times she'd probably have welcomed such an escape.

Like other women in similar situations, in the days before social help programs, she had learned to get by. Ingeniously, she had stretched food, had made clothes from flour sacks, and had doctored with herbs and whatever she could gather around the house. After many years of living like this, money, understandably, was rightfully respected and, for the rest of her life, spent carefully.

One day late in her long life, she was at the doctor's office when the nurse appeared with a small cup and asked Nano for a urine sample. Nano grumpily took the small cup and eyed it suspiciously.

"Ain't you got nothin' bigger than this?" She handed the paper cup back to the nurse. "I don't know that I can hit this."

The nurse responded, "Well, yes we do. I can get something

else, but there'll be a twelve-dollar charge for it and this cup is free."

Quick as a flash, Nano, as stingy a woman as God ever did make, snatched the cup back. *"Give me that cup!* For twelve dollars, I could hit a thimble!"

And she meant it.

Not surprisingly, when she died, this woman who had spent most of her days struggling for every penny, left behind money, land, and property. From nothing, she had been able to produce a good bit of something.

The Great Depression turned out to be a mighty fine teacher to those who lived through it. They were mindful that what had happened once could happen again, so they wanted to be prepared. Just in case. After decades of prosperity and easy credit, too many people have lost a healthy respect for what people in the hard-hit mountains often called, "the almighty dollar." People, though, who have respect for every dollar earned will never find themselves without one. It's that simple. The biggest factors for extreme stress, the kinds that keep people awake at night, are health problems and money issues. While many health issues are unavoidable, many money problems, on the other hand, could have been avoided. I decided many years ago that I had enough stresses that are inescapable without adding money worries.

My parents were mindful of every dollar earned, not for how much they could spend but how much they could save. Mama would carefully count money, holding it as though each bill were rare and precious. She wanted me to go to college and better myself during a time when the only way was scholarships or cash. No one borrowed money for higher education. If you couldn't afford it, you got a job instead. To see to it that her child was well educated, she took in sewing. She charged twenty-five dollars for a dress that would take most of two days to make. Every twenty-five dollars added up, so she managed to save enough money to pay for my tuition and books at an expensive private college. Most students on campus came from wealthy families who didn't blink at writing a check when tuition was due, but Mama, on the other hand, counted her money at the end of every week. She knew how much she had to have every three months in order to pay for my college bills. Without fail, she had it. It was a formidable accomplishment, one I especially appreciate these days when I listen to radio financial hosts who counsel an endless stream of folks who exit college with tremendous debt.

"You have to give up a lot of little things in order to have the big things," she said frequently. Once when I was in junior high, we were shopping and I found a set of sheets on sale that she had been wanting for quite some time. Excited, I ran to find her and share the good news.

She nodded and said nothing. I persisted. "I'm not goin' to get them today," she finally said.

"Why not? They're on sale and you said you would get them when they went on sale." I was incredulous.

"I can't afford them today." She paused. "I might be able to afford them better another day when they're not on sale than I can afford them today."

That's pretty smart. We often justify a purchase because it's on sale when, in truth, we can't afford it any more than if it weren't on sale.

In the early years after college graduation, I got caught up in the headiness of a paycheck and being able to purchase store-bought clothes after a lifetime of wearing homemade dresses.

Saving money never crossed my mind. As inevitably happens with such a flippant attitude toward finances, I got in a pinch. It took a year or two to get all the credit card debt paid off but when it was over, I was a changed person. I never charge more than I can pay off at the end of the month, and I save out of every dollar earned. Even if I can only put five dollars aside, I do it because it's a discipline and keeps me in the habit of saving. If I want something special, I save particularly for it rather than taking it from a savings account. In addition to an overall savings account, I always keep three mortgage payments in another account. Over the years, I have worked part-time jobs in addition to full-time employment in order to have "extras," driven cars until they had over 200,000 miles on them, and deprived myself of luxury items when I could not afford them.

In return, I sleep well at night and, boy, I do love my sleep. When the economy took a nosedive and my business, like most, slowed, I did not have the additional worry of how to pay my bills. I had saved during the prosperous times and knew it would get me through the hard times until a better day returned. There was never any doubt in my mind that a better day was coming. I just had to wade through the tough days to get there. In truth, I can't remember the details of one dress that I have passed over or one knickknack I have not bought for my house in order to save the money. Resisting those unimportant purchases had enabled me to have the luxury of peace of mind when revenue was uncertain.

Frugality is an undervalued virtue. In days of prosperity, frugality is often considered frivolous. Why save or even manage spending when there is so much to be bought? Why bother with coupons or negotiation or watching sales? Here's the best reason in the world: When an economic downturn comes—and it always comes, whether it's on a national level or personal one—stress is greatly reduced by the comfort of a savings account and manageable debt.

There are many stressful events and situations that we have no control over in life—death, health issues, relationship problems, roofs that suddenly spring a leak during a terrible storm—but financial worries can be tremendously reduced by planning for a rainy day. By saving, you control more of your future and circumstances. As Daddy often intoned, "Don't get yourself so in debt that you become enslaved to a job you hate just to pay your bills." Once you've been in that position, you never want to be there again. Few things are worse in life than knowing you cannot afford to quit a job that makes you miserable. It makes a bad situation into a desperate one.

Here's a simple formula to follow and one that should be taught to children from an early age: Out of every dollar, give away 10 percent and save 10 percent. If you do that, you'll be surprised at how much further the rest of the money goes.

You'll also be delighted at how much better you sleep every night without money worries hanging over your head.

CHAPTER 29:

Find the Beauty and Success in Your Life and Rejoice in It

robably nothing causes more distress, depression, and unhappiness than people who are always judging their lives against others, wishing for greater success. Daddy used to say, "No matter how good you are at something, there's always someone who's better." On the same line, there's always someone who's going to have more than you have—a bigger house, a more expensive car, more professional accolades, or prettier eyes. If you dwell on what someone else has or has accomplished, you'll drive yourself into depression. After all, you have things that those other people probably want. No life is perfect, but every life has beauty and success. It's a shame to waste time dwelling on what isn't rather than the beauty of what is.

Mama had a simple life, one that looked boringly ordinary and remarkably unaccomplished. I seriously doubt that if her life had been offered in trade, that anyone would have taken it. For most of her life, she was a stay-at-home mother, a "homemaker" is what she proudly called herself. Without question, she worked as hard as Daddy and probably, if the truth be told, even harder. After she married, she only worked outside of the house for three years and that was to help Daddy pay his way out of a debt when a dishonest employee had stolen from him. Yet, she was the best at what she did, and she did it with great thought. She cooked a hot breakfast every morning, complete with homemade biscuits, a hot supper every night, and she was always wherever her husband or children needed her to be. Money was never in abundance, yet she managed each penny until it turned into a dime. Daddy worked hard to make ends meet, but she kept those ends tied in a hard knot. Even to me, it looked like a pretty mundane, even boring life. It certainly wasn't my idea of an enjoyable life.

But Mama showed me different.

"I'm so proud of my children," she said suddenly one day as we were driving along. "You've all done so well and accomplished so much." She paused. "You know I was raised to believe that you just did the best you could. It never occurred to me that I could have gone out into the world and done the big things I've seen my children do." Then she stopped and smiled brightly. "But I've had the best life. No one's had a better life than me."

I was so surprised that I spun my head around and looked at her. "Really? You wouldn't change anything about your life?"

"No ma'am," she replied firmly. "I've had everything I ever wanted in life. When I was growing up, all I wanted was to be a wife and mother. I never thought of anything else. I had a wonderful husband for fifty-eight years who loved me and four healthy, nice children. I wouldn't trade my life for anyone else's."

Mama never had anything fancy. She sewed most of her own clothes, and there were many weeks of her life when she only left the house on Sunday morning for church, staying at home the other six days. My parents took only one vacation in their entire lives—to visit relatives one summer. It was such a big deal that as we planned for the trip, Mama thought we should lock our house for those two weeks. My parents had built the house about fifteen years before, and in that time, had never locked any of the outside doors. To appease Mama, Daddy searched high and low for a key but to no avail. There was no choice but to leave the doors unlocked for fifteen days and, of course, nothing happened while we were gone.

Until she was widowed and began to travel with me occasionally, she had stayed no more than six or seven nights in a motel in her eight decades. Yet, she loved her life, appreciated what was blessed about it, and did not compare it to anyone else's. Because of that attitude, she lived a content, peaceful existence. If she had spent time looking at what others had that she didn't, she would have been miserable. Yet, she was smart enough to see that her simple life had solid rewards—she was content to add value to the lives of her family members and enjoy it.

You know the most interesting thing about that conversation with Mama? The next afternoon, less than twenty-four hours after she made those remarks, she died unexpectedly from a brain aneurysm at the age of eighty-seven. She had arrived at my house for a birthday party and came in the front door, chatting merrily. She told a little family story, then tossed a point from her forefinger, laughed gaily, and said, "And don't you forget that." Then she swayed, trying to catch her balance before falling to the floor. She was gone. Her last words had been a fond family story, and her last emotion had been laughter. She was happily content with her life until the end. No comparisons. No regrets. Nothing could be more beautiful than that.

My friend Michelle is beautiful, kind, and well educated. She has chosen to be a stay-at-home mom to her only child, a son who she had welcomed after years of desiring a family. He is her most cherished blessing, so she doesn't want to miss a moment with him. Her days are spent in carpool, school activities, and study lessons. Simple days, really. One morning I opened an e-mail from her sent the previous night before bedtime that began, "I have had the greatest day." Whenever someone says something like that, it usually means that a big refund came from the IRS or another unbelievable piece of good news had come. Not with Michelle, who wrote of the sweet joy of her day of simply taking her child to school, having lunch with a dear friend, running various errands, helping out a friend, retrieving her preschooler, then coming home to discover that her husband had surprised her by leaving work early. "It has been such a lovely day." She had served others as well as delighted in the small joys.

Thusly inspired by her ability to rejoice in simple pleasures, I promptly decided to do something that is innately against my workaholic nature: I took the day off. It was darkly clouded and rainy, so I put on comfortable clothes, made a dish of my decadent, calorie-loaded macaroni and cheese (I gave myself a day off from counting calories, a big treat in itself), pulled a good book from a stack of many waiting to be read, built a fire, and snuggled in for the joy of a simple day. To the outside world, no doubt it would have appeared uneventful and unmemorable. But I found beauty and joy in it, and I celebrated it. By refreshing myself, I was able to do better work the next day and to be kinder and more compassionate to others because I wasn't stressed.

"Do you like your job?" I asked curiously to the cheerful woman who, despite her large girth, was able to flit easily around the dining table and see to the needs of several elderly residents of the nursing home. I had come by to visit my friends, Guy and Pinky, a devoted couple in their eighties who had suffered health setbacks that cost them their independent living. But they were happily together, so it mattered not to them that they had gone from a comfortable, three-bedroom, two-bath home to a tiny one bedroom with a tinier sitting area. Life had changed for them, but they were still together and that was all that mattered. In the dining room, I had pulled up a chair and waited with them as their meal was served.

The woman, probably in her late thirties, greeted each diner with a beautiful chirp and acknowledged their personal dietary requirements.

"Okay, Mr. Guy, here is your roast beef all blended for you." She pulled the cover from the dish. "And we got chocolate puddin' for dessert. I knows that's your favorite."

To another who could not speak and appeared to barely realize he was in the world, she said, "Now, Mr. Henry, you know how we've talked about you drinkin' your protein shake. Ain't that right?"

He blinked his eyes and she grinned. "That's my pal. You drink it just for me. All rightee?" He took the straw in his mouth that she offered. She patted him on the shoulder. "You a fine man. Yes, siree, you sure is."

I was impressed. Not with just how good she was at her job but that she did it cheerfully and, without a doubt, she probably made no more than minimum wage. It's a hard job for little money. I wondered if she was just pretending, so I asked how she liked her job.

"Oh, I love my job. I love all these wonderful people. They need me and I make a difference in their life."

"She's good," Pinky commented. "She does a wonderful job."

I smiled. "How long have you been here?"

She was unrolling a napkin but looked up for a moment. "Well, 'bout six months but I worked at another nursin' home for 'bout seven years before I come here."

"You're so kind," I said.

"Thank ya," she said with a smile. "This is my callin', though. I knows I help with these folks and that lifts my spirits. Yes, indeed."

Now, a lot of people wouldn't find joy in a job that pays little, requires standing up for eight or nine hours, or offers few, if any, opportunities for advancement. Yet, that lovely woman realized she was an enormous blessing to folks in their twilight years. She seized the opportunity, determined to give it all she could. She found happiness in a simple, hard-working life, and in the bargain, she was making an important difference.

Finding a better day sometime is as uncomplicated as being a better person because of the simple pleasures of life, like serving others when the opportunity arises.

CHAPTER 30:

Everything Works Out If You Let It

The e-mail request that came from a reader seeking my advice was frantic and fraught with despair. The words jumped off the screen with the kind of hopelessness that must surely be felt by a man standing on a ledge, debating whether to jump or not.

The young woman explained that she had been engaged to a soldier who had just deployed to a war zone. Shortly before he left, he had broken the engagement because of the endless conflicts between his fiancée and his mother. She was very angry, mainly because she believed that his mother had badgered him to end their engagement. Aside from anger, she was completely heartbroken. She had tried repeatedly—through phone calls, texts, and endless e-mails—to contact him, but he refused all communication. She was desperate to talk to him and, importantly, restore their engagement.

"Oh, please," she begged. "Tell me what to do. I'll do anything you say."

"It's quite simple," I wrote in reply. "Leave him alone and he'll come back. Stop pestering him and give him time to think about missing you. He'll be back."

That wasn't the advice she wanted, so she argued against it. Mainly, she explained, she was so hurt and unhappy that she couldn't just step back and wait. She couldn't bear the pain, she said. She had to work it out right then, as soon as possible.

"Listen," I replied, a bit irritated that she had vowed to do whatever I said but now was arguing against it. "If you don't step back and leave him alone, your pain is just beginning. It will never end. I promise you this—if you will fall silent, he will come back."

She finally managed to overcome herself enough to do just as I instructed. And, it worked. In less than two weeks, he called to say he couldn't live without her. The engagement was reinstated. She was ecstatic when she delivered the news. I left her with one last bit of advice: find a way to get along with his mother. Otherwise, you're creating a lifetime of needless problems for yourself and you're putting the man you love in a position where he will always be torn between the two women he loves the most.

How did I know that he would come back? First of all, a soldier in a war zone has incredible clarity of mind and heart. He views things much differently than those who are safe and secure. I had little doubt that once he looked death in the eye every day, he would see quickly the importance of love. But, soldier or not, it's the same advice I give to any woman who is facing a crisis of the heart where her man has walked away. If there is not something fundamentally wrong in the relationship, such as betrayal, an addiction, or an extreme unkindness, the man will come back, either immediately or eventually. But he has to be left alone to sort out his thoughts and fully experience his heart, then he will decide for himself. The more a woman pushes, the farther away she drives him. Too much pushing and he will be gone. Forever.

A man, though, cannot stand the sound of silence. He also needs the opportunity to "miss" a woman, but if she keeps pestering him and pleading with him to come back, she has stolen the very opportunity that will return him to her. She hasn't given him time to miss her. So in other words, don't meddle. While it does have a place in our own lives and sometimes in the lives of others, too often meddling is unnecessary. It falls far short of fixing things, and usually makes situations much worse. Yes, we have to be proactive in our lives. We have to take charge of finances, health, or career paths, but there's a fine line between doing enough and doing too much. Once you've crossed that line, you're meddling.

Compare it, if you will, to making a pot of vegetable soup. You choose the best vegetables, chop them, make a nice tomato base, then you taste it. Hmmm, it needs a bit more salt. And then a dash more. If you're not careful, you'll cross the line into meddling too much. Then, the soup is too salty and uneatable. Have you ever tried taking salt out of food? It's impossible. You have to know when to stop, both with soup and situations. Sometimes you can't undo the damage you do.

One tremendous stress we can face is trouble in the work place with colleagues who are challenging. Unfortunately, some people do not learn to play well with others while in kindergarten, so they carry their lack of social skills into the workplace. It can be downright painful to those with whom they work. Over coffee one day, I noticed that a longtime friend was weary and sad-looking. She lacked her usual spark and enthusiasm.

"What's wrong?" I finally asked. "It's obvious that you have some kind of strong worry."

She looked down at her coffee and shook her head. "It's work."

"Work?" I was momentarily stunned. She had always loved her job in public relations, to the point that she happily worked long hours and rarely took vacation. She lived to work. "What's wrong?"

After years with the same company where she had been treasured and well rewarded, she now felt insecure and troubled. She left the office each day as soon as possible, counted the hours until Friday afternoon, then on Sunday afternoon began dreading Monday morning. Her dream job had become a nightmare, and it was all due to a young woman who had been hired directly out of college several months earlier. Once she started talking, she couldn't stop. She gave a diatribe on her conniving coworker whose charming façade had the bosses fooled. They thought her the perfect employee while, behind their backs, she created strife with others and plotted, in particular, to undermine my friend.

"It's like that movie, *All About Eve*," she said. "I befriended her and set out to mentor her, but she has turned on me and is doing her best to get my job. She's very clever about it, so upper management doesn't see her tactics. It took me twelve years of hard work to get here; now she thinks she can just come in and steal it out from under me." She rubbed her temples. "The sad but awful truth is that it's working. It's obvious that the boss favors her. I've been reprimanded for not being a good team player!"

My friend, in an effort to stand up for herself, had spoken directly to the young woman about her devious ways. Rather than help the situation, it had hurt it because the troublemaker had high-tailed it immediately to the boss's office, and with tears pooling in her eyes, had portrayed my friend as a jealous, malicious older woman who was trying to stomp on an innocent soul. From that moment forth, things had spun out of control. My friend lost favor, and as she rightfully tried to save her hard-won territory, she appeared desperate. The constant worry and looking over her shoulder at the enemy had caused her work to suffer noticeably, a fact that had been duly noted in her most recent job review.

"Okay," I began. "You're not going to like what I have to say but listen anyway." She bit her lower lip, waiting for the advice. I once faced a similar situation, and I made the same mistakes that she did. Finally, I found what worked. "Ignore her. Leave her alone. Focus on your work and getting your job done. Stop trying to fix things. Let things fix themselves."

"If I leave her alone, she'll eat me up!" she exclaimed. "I'll be shredded to pieces."

I shook my head. "That's what you're doing to yourself now. She's smart enough that she's luring you into destroying yourself. She set you up, and you've played into her hands. But if you leave her alone, she will eventually trip herself up and who she is will all come to light. Trust me on this—deceptive, manipulative people always reveal who they are. Always. Back off and stop trying to fix this yourself. Take back the upper hand by taking the high road."

The hard part about being pushed to that point of desperation is reeling yourself back in and regaining control. My friend, bright woman that she is, listened. Oh, she argued and debated it for a couple of weeks, but eventually, she gave it a try. Her nemesis was completely thrown off by the change in tactic. My friend made public overtures to her, complimented her in front of the boss, and most importantly, left her alone while she returned to concentrating on her work and doing the quality job for which she had long been known.

One day, the young employee overslept and missed a major event that had been her assignment. When the boss finally managed to get the sleeping girl to answer her phone and it was clear that she could not make it to the event in time, my friend stepped in and flawlessly managed it to conclusion. The tide turned. My friend regained the upper hand.

The interesting thing about conniving folks is that once they stumble as this girl did, they have an almost impossible time regaining their footing. It was downhill rather steadily for the girl, who left the company about a year later. She moved on to another company where the boss—an intuitive female—quickly saw through her wily ways when she tried the same tactics with her new coworkers. The instinctive boss reined in the troublesome employee. The young woman, who knew no other way to operate, left that job within a year and eventually drifted away. No one knows where she is or what happened to her.

My friend, however, is a huge success and is well known in her field of work. Though she was temporarily sidetracked (and almost sidelined permanently), she found the point where she should stop meddling. As a result, everything worked out beautifully.

Don't be a full-time fixer. Accept the fact that some things just have to run their course, creating new opportunities, building character, and providing experience. Situations have a way of working out, and they can do it quicker and better if left alone.

Sometimes the best way to manage a problem is to manage your own meddling.

CHAPTER 31:

To Ponder Deeply Is to Learn Exponentially

The busyness of the world today has resulted in the loss of pondering, which is the ability to look deeply at situations around us and, therefore, gain wisdom. Distractions abound, driven mostly by technology, which keeps us continually distracted by communication. Unless we make a concentrated effort to put away smartphones for a while every day, we miss valuable opportunities to look and learn. Most people in today's society think "automatically" because they're multitasking. They're on the phone while picking up the mail or yelling at the kids while putting away the groceries. Ever have a moment when you can't remember where you put something or you can't remember if you did something or not? You weren't thinking about it when you did it, so your memory couldn't store it.

Beyond our normal memory needs, nothing benefits us more in life than pondering situations, sifting through them until we acquire wisdom and knowledge. We don't have to live it to learn it. We can learn from others. But, first, we have to be conscious to take the time to stop and turn it over in our minds.

As a reporter, I covered a couple of stories that, at the time, made me stop in my tracks and think about choices we make in life. When I first started my newspaper career, I stumbled across a twenty-year-old newspaper article about a local eighteen-year-old boy who had bravely darted in front of a train to rescue a two-year-old who had toddled into danger. Witnesses reported that it had been a harrowing feat of heroism, and as a result, had nominated the teenager for the Carnegie Award for Heroism. He had been honored with a medal and a nice sum of money, which had helped him to go to college. True to who he was, he had become an engineer, had gotten married, had started a family, and had continued to make a difference.

I pitched the idea of reuniting the two and my editor enthusiastically agreed, so I set about tracking down both men. The Carnegie hero originally said no, primarily because he was a modest man who didn't want the spotlight. A few days later, he called back and said that he had changed his mind. He was curious to see what had become of the life he had saved.

I arrived at the tiny, rundown house where the rescued baby, by then a twenty-two-year-old, lived with his parents. He appeared stoned, was jobless, disheveled, unclean, and, to my mind, an example of wasted humanity. I was still trying to adjust to the shock of the situation when the hero, dressed in perfectly pressed trousers and starched shirt, arrived. I was not much more than a kid, but I was mature enough to absorb the drama of the moment. The look of woeful disappointment on the hero's face was vivid when he stepped up on the porch and saw the wasted life he had once risked his own to save. In two seconds, I had successfully managed to shatter the optimistic hope that the hero had carried for two decades. He had probably envisioned the rescued baby paying forward his own generosity and helping others; instead, he discovered a selfish person who lived only for personal desire and gratification. That moment of crystallization taught me how we can learn from others—both good and bad—if only we look and ponder. I saw good from the hero and how he had conducted his life. There was sadness in the other life. It had been spared by a young man willing to risk his life yet squandered by the one saved. What a stark comparison of lives.

Another time, I was doing a story on a hometown hero who had been a stellar high school athlete, had set college football records, and had gone on to play professionally, even winning a Super Bowl ring. He was long retired, so I was writing a story on his life after football. I interviewed him over the phone and as we were concluding the call, I asked, "Would it be possible to get a couple of photos of you when you were in high school?"

"Sure," he replied. "Call my dad. He has all that."

The athlete had grown up in a wealthy family. They lived in a beautiful home and the son, good-looking as well as talented, had driven an expensive car while in high school. Knowing this, I was surprised when I called the dad and he gave me directions to his home. It was near the railroad tracks, a landmark that truly separated the haves from the have-nots. Bewildered, I turned my car into the parking lot of the address he had given me. It was a rundown strip shopping center with four tiny store areas, long abandoned by commerce or traffic.

"This can't possibly be it," I muttered to myself. On the glass front door, I saw the address he had given me. I decided to get out of the car and ask. My knock was answered by a weathered old man, hunched slightly, who smiled when he saw me.

"Right on time," he said approvingly. "Come in."

Speechless, I walked into the tiny one room that had formerly been a retail store. A glance around revealed a hot plate, a percolator, empty bottles of booze, a disheveled daybed with a rough-looking brown chenille spread, and a black-and-white television playing a game show. He walked over to the daybed, got down on his knees, reached in, and pulled out a shoebox.

"Sit here," he motioned to the daybed, standing up. With trembling hands made so by the evil of alcohol, he took off the lid and began sifting through pieces of yesterday's glory. It was my first up close and personal look at how someone on top of the world can tumble to harrowing depths, and it had a profound effect on me. I pondered it deeply for years, coming to the conclusion that good days have to be protected. Otherwise, they can be thrown away carelessly and destroy any hope of better days to come.

The most arrogant mistake we can make in life is to believe that the blessings of good fortune and prosperity will last forever, to think that once we've made it professionally, financially, and personally, that there is no going back. Wrong. We can go back even farther than the place from which we started. One phone call, one dramatically wrong choice, or one doctor's diagnosis can reverse good and cause lives to slam into bad. The wise live each day, grateful and humbled while mindful of the importance of each decision, large or small.

From all of my pondering I've learned: Good fortune tempts arrogance, arrogance gives birth to a feeling of invincibility which, in turn, brings insouciance to decision-making, and the next step can be downward mobility. It's destruction, a devastating leveling of an enviable and once powerful life. We should never take for granted a good marriage, health, a steady job, or other piece of good fortune. Handle each day with the same kind of careful appraisal and thoughtfulness as the younger days when we chose colleges, jobs, or a wedding dress. That is the key mistake of many: decisions are sometimes made with a shrug and an airiness driven by a false sense of security.

From others, we can learn to make strategic steps to avoid their mistakes or emulate their successes. That old man, once prosperous and successful, lived out the remainder of his life like that. He died a drunk, forsaken and cast off by most who had once reveled in his glory. There was a powerful lesson to learn from that, and while I, just a stranger, saw the lesson, his son did not. Several years later, the athlete, once a Heisman contender, was found alone at home, days after he died suddenly. Though he had known fame and riches, he wound up with serious troubles of his own. His life had mimicked his father in both glory and sorrow. As F. Scott Fitzgerald once said, "Show me a hero and I'll write you a tragedy."

Had the son pondered the fate that befell his dad, he might have been able to avoid a troublesome path. I often think about the outcome of a friend, and it keeps me mindful of how a twist of fate, seemingly unimportant at the time, can sneak up on you and steal the fruits of your life.

I met Beth when we were both sports writers. She worked

for a major paper and eventually went to work for a national newspaper. She was a hard worker, talented, lovely, and a good, decent person. We were close friends, united by the fact that we were two-of-a-kind working in a man's world. Through her diligence, she earned the top motorsports reporting position in the nation. Shortly after, she fell in love with "the most terrific guy in the world," and all was well. I was so proud of her. She had everything going for her. Perhaps, I was even a little envious. Her life was close to perfection.

One day, she was playing a Celebrity Pro-Am golf tournament when she tee'ed the ball up and took a swing, nothing unusual other than she turned in a way that twisted her back and she crumbled to her knees in agony. As life events go, a simple twist of the back could seem unremarkable. After all, it wasn't a devastating car wreck or a terminal disease.

It was, though, the bland, nondescript beginning to the end. Despite surgeries and physical therapy, she could not escape the constant pain. She became addicted to painkillers, lost her job, and the "most terrific guy in the world" left her. She began combining pills with alcohol. For the last ten years of her life, she knew no happiness or peace. She died too young. A great life which she had worked hard to put together had been taken by a quiet thief who had sneaked up, caught her off guard, then had stolen everything little by little.

When Beth died, I came to this conclusion: It's not the big setbacks that are most likely to destroy our lives because we steel ourselves and take on those challenges like a house that is lost to a natural disaster, a divorce, or the death of a loved one. We know those are big challenges, so we gird ourselves, then forge headlong into them and fight those battles. It's the seemingly inconsequential ones—like a back injury while golfing—that can rock our worlds and take everything from us if we do not stay alert. These small twists of fate can be insidious, leading us to the wrong turn. We don't even realize it until we see the wrong destination looming ahead. Sometimes, it's too late to turn around.

I was profoundly touched by what I saw happen in the life of a good friend. And, now, thanks to my proclivity for pondering, I have discovered a lesson that will keep me cautious and alert down through the journey of my life. I am now mindful to watch the small turns in the road as carefully as the big, deep curves. It is something we should all remember: be mindful to protect the future, so you can collect all the better days that lie ahead.

CHAPTER 32:

You Can Go Anywhere in Life, Regardless of Where You Begin

A s childhoods go, my cousin, Ricky, did not have an idyllic one, certainly not one to be envied. It was hard, dirt poor, and definitely not the kind that's considered a strong springboard into a bright future. It was underprivileged and, sadly, was what is still considered normal by some families in the Appalachian Mountains.

When Ricky was two years old, his mama packed up her three small children, left her boozing, gambling husband, and moved in with my grandparents and simple-minded aunt. In a

tiny, four-room, tin-roofed house with no indoor plumbing
where they were forced to sleep three and four to a bedroom
and keep warm with a wood-burning stove and handmade
quilts, Ricky spent his life until he was eighteen and struck out
on his own.

Despite his lack of a father's love or creature comforts, he
was always a sweet boy with an easy smile who showed no anger
or bitterness over his situation. Our Sunday afternoons after
church and dinner were often spent with a group of cousins
playing in the swimming hole or inventing games to entertain
ourselves. While some might feel sorry for such a sparse
upbringing, Ricky will be quick to tell you that it helped to make
him into the successful man he became. He wanted to do better
than what he had seen his daddy do. See, a certain amount of
want in a child has a way of creating an unstoppable drive to
have a better life, to make a living good enough to avoid living
like that again. A child raised in the lap of luxury and given
everything will never have the same kind of determination as
Ricky has because they don't know the sting of deprivation and
the hollowness of just barely getting by.

Early on, he showed ingenuity and drive. Around the age of
twelve, he rode his raggedy red, secondhand bike around to
trash piles and retrieved gallon milk jugs. He washed them, then
sold them to moonshiners, who used them to store their brew,
for twenty-five cents apiece, once selling a thousand of them.

Our grandmother, a God-fearing woman, laid down the
law. "Ain't no whiskey maker gonna pull up in this yard and get
'em," she railed. Ricky, respectful but undeterred, strung the
milk jugs together, tied them to the handles of his bike and rode
off to meet the moonshiner at an agreed destination.

"Once I got twenty-five dollars, and that was so much

money to me," he said. "I used to keep it in a cigar box under the bed. By the time I was fifteen, I had about seven or eight hundred dollars."

He was such a thinker and hard worker that, early on, there was no doubt that he was going to make a different life for his family than what he had known. Like many in similar situations in the Appalachians, he quit high school as soon as he got old enough (though he eventually studied and tested to get his diploma, he regrets that) and went to work on a chicken farm that included a hatchery. By the time he was twenty and had a wife and young son, through eighty- and hundred-hour workweeks, he had become the hatchery manager. Within a few years, he moved to a company that made roller bearings. It was a decent job with good benefits but, as he explained, "I got tired of being just a number to them."

In every successful life that has a bridge between poverty and prosperity, there is a turning point. For Ricky, it came the day he had to borrow five dollars to see him through to pay day two weeks later.

"I thought to myself, 'What am I doin'?' I was always behind and tryin' to catch up. I knew I didn't want to live out my life like that. I wanted to get ahead." A familiar sweet smile crossed his face. "I was tired of losin'."

When he was ten, Ricky built a tree house out in the woods. I have no idea what the inside looked like because "Girls Weren't Allowed." At the time he didn't realize it, but that was his calling—building houses. The calling of our lives always appears during childhood. We only have to look back and, clearly, we will see it.

He left the factory and took a job on a framing crew, an apprenticeship of sorts, and spent the next few years learning the craft. He built two speculation "spec" houses. On one he made money but on the other lost $10,000, more than he had made on the other one. In the end, that loss turned out to be one of the best investments of his life.

"I learned from that mistake. I learned how to make money on houses because I found how I could modify plans by making them the most accessible and efficient. That's the mistake that people make—they give up easily." Ricky dug in, worked hard, and prayed harder. "I knew I couldn't do it without God's help." On his next spec, he made $10,000, but the bank made the same amount in interest. That set him to thinking.

"I saw real quick that the more you could keep a bank out of it, the more money you could make." In addition to the spec houses, he—and eventually his son, Greg—built custom houses and bought rental properties, always relying heavily on cash rather than borrowed money. They naturally segued into developing subdivisions, continuing to roll cash forward into projects. As a result, when the nation experienced a virtual dead stop in home construction and homebuilders collapsed in droves, Ricky and Greg did not sway. They were smartly prepared to weather the raging storm. Not only had they made millions, they had saved it, too.

"It's not what you make that counts," Ricky pointed out. "It's how you spend what you make."

An acquaintance spoke of how he had made a low-ball offer on a stunningly beautiful lot in one of Ricky's subdivisions, thinking that, like most developers, he was hurting for cash and would snap up the money. "No, thank you," replied Ricky's son, Greg. "We don't owe anything on these, so we can just wait it out until the market comes back."

With resourcefulness and determination, Ricky managed to

bring financial destiny into his control rather than being controlled by it. Borrowing that five dollars was exactly the rude awakening that he needed.

"I grew up hard and fast," he said softly. "I got pushed around and bullied probably because I was poor. I didn't want my kids to have that kind of life."

He laughed lightly. "I remember your daddy tellin' me once that hard work never killed no one. He was right, but I did get awfully tired."

Ricky started life with no advantages, but he didn't settle. Through various twists and turns, he came to realize that a humble mountain house, not much more than a shack, without heat or plumbing might have been his beginning, but it did not have to be his end. From that little place with the red dirt yard where chickens scratched around, he could go anywhere. He just had a farther way to travel than some people.

"Kids today," he shook his head. "They lose the value of accomplishment because things come easy for them. That's a sad thing. I know if I'm gonna have something, I'm gonna work for it. That's fine with me."

His philosophy is simple: never take your profits and stay away from the addiction of greed. "If you're not careful, the more you have, the more you'll want. You'll get addicted to money."

Even in recent times when he has spent more in property taxes than he has produced in income, he is confident of a financial turnaround. "I know there are better days out there. There are always better days. You just have to have the vision to believe in the future."

He's right. The future is limited only by our vision and our dreams. It is not limited by the circumstances of where we began or where we are now. You can go anywhere from any starting point. Sometimes the way is just longer than others, but it can be done. It can always be done.

CHAPTER 33:

The Easy Way Out Often Turns Out to Be the Hardest

L ife is so challenging that it's a natural propensity for any of us to choose easy over hard. After all, if you were driving through a traffic-jammed city like Los Angeles or Atlanta, wouldn't you pick the route with the fewest stops and starts? The streets where the driving is easy and not stressful?

But life doesn't work like that. Sometimes we have to choose the harder way of two choices because if we don't, the easy way will eventually lead to a much harder path to travel. It is during these times that we have to will ourselves toward the path of immediate discomfort and away from what appears to be a beautiful path of pleasure. Now, that's difficult. It is humanly normal to be pulled toward pleasure and away from pain. No one wants to hurt. We want to feel good every moment that it's possible. Discipline, though, beats regret.

I knew a woman once who adored the ground her husband walked on. You can't imagine a couple happier than those two people. They were in their mid-thirties, had been married for ten years, and had chosen to have no children so that they could devote themselves completely to each other, something they did with daily joy. Every time she mentioned him, she glowed. It was the kind of relationship that everyone envies, a fairy tale come true.

They were building their dream home on a gorgeous piece of property that had a river and large, beautiful trees. One Saturday morning, it was raining hard, but Josh needed to go out to the new house and meet with the builder. En route, his SUV hydroplaned on the wet pavement and hit a guard rail. He was killed instantly. His wife was devastated. It was one of the most heartrending situations I've ever experienced. She was inconsolable.

About two months after Josh was killed, she met a widower with three school-age children. They connected over their mutual grief and began to be drawn together. She felt pleasure in his attraction to her and that pleasure helped to mask the intense pain she was experiencing. Six weeks after they met, they announced their engagement, and despite friends' warnings, she turned a deaf ear and married him quickly.

"Josh, though I loved him mightily, is gone. I must move on. This is a good man, and he brings me joy," she said. "Just be happy for me after all I've faced." Her words I knew were shallow, but she had convinced herself to believe them and thought by taking that road, which felt better than the sorrow, she would escape the pain.

"Marry in haste, repent in leisure," wise Mama used to say. The marriage lasted less than a year and, suddenly, she didn't have just one husband to heal over, she had two. On top of tremendous hurt, she had piled more hurt. Additionally, she was embarrassed over her impulsiveness and was deeply sorrowed because she believed that she had blatantly disregarded the importance of Josh and had done an injustice to his memory. She would have given anything to take back that hasty marriage because it only added to the pain and suffering of her enormous loss.

For a brief moment, she had been drawn toward pleasure and away from pain. By not taking the time to allow her heart and spirit to recover, she added incalculable sorrow and regret. The easy way became the hardest way. The pain was great and she was suffering emotionally, so she looked for a quick fix that she thought would last forever. Probably if she had listened to her deep gut instinct instead of reacting emotionally, she would have avoided greater pain.

In retrospect, she should have fought the heavy traffic on that highway of suffering despite the length and difficulty of the journey. She would have recovered more quickly and completely. One of the strongest truths of life is that happiness teaches us nothing but sorrow teaches us everything. From the wisdom we gain while traveling the unpaved road with ruts, we will make fewer future mistakes, and therefore, not have to look for any way out—easy or hard.

It's a deceiving trap to fall into, in all kinds of situations. I had a job once that was about 50 percent miserable. There were good things about the job in that I was paid well, traveled extensively, liked many of my responsibilities, and had good friends in the office. On the other hand, I didn't like the city in which I lived, I was a long way from my family, and I had a tyrannical boss who yelled and cussed at me a lot. Not just me, but anyone who drew his displeasure. I had never been treated that way, and I didn't adapt well to it. My spirit was crushed. I often came back to my small one-bedroom apartment and cried.

One day, a similar company in a city closer to home called and began to court me. The manager of the rival company offered more money and welcomed words of encouragement. I didn't look twice or think. I leaped at the opportunity. In my youthful exuberance, it never occurred to me that I could get into a worse situation. Suddenly, I went from being 50 percent miserable to being 100 percent miserable. I was looking for an easy way out of a hard place and as Mama had often warned: I jumped from the frying pan into the fire.

The good times in the new job lasted about two weeks, then the boss with the sweet words became a master devil. My heaven became my hell. Mail was opened and read before it was brought to me, usually with comments noted on the correspondence—this still astonishes me—my phone messages were intercepted, and it was considered acceptable to listen in on private phone calls. There was no trust or freedom. I had no friends there because everyone was paranoid from similar treatment, so there was constant conniving and backbiting. By accident, I discovered the company was possibly engaged in legally questionable practices. After a few months, I escaped by quitting. The easy way out had failed miserably, and I was in a much harder place because I didn't have a job for several months.

Simply put, there's no quick fixes to tough situations. The tougher a situation is, the longer it takes to work out, but with perseverance, it can be managed and overcome. It requires determination and just diving in to repair it with persistent tenacity. As Shakespeare wrote, "Much rain wears the marble." Easy ways out are reserved for inconsequential events in life like finding a way to duck out of a family gathering that you dread in favor of doing something you enjoy or finding a short cut to a difficult recipe. We reach the deepest level of maturity when we are able to pull our shoulders back, take a deep breath, cover our minds with determination, and plunge in to taking the hard way, resisting all enticements to veer over to the easy way.

Now whenever I'm tempted, I think of the little screen that comes up when rebooting my satellite system that displays the progress where a bar will show 10 percent completed, 20, 50, and so forth. Usually, it gets to 99 percent and takes an abnormally long time to finish the process. I get anxious, but I know that if I interrupt it before it is 100 percent complete, I'll have to start all over again. Then, it will take even more time and effort. There isn't an easy way out. So I wait until it is completely finished.

It's the same with many situations in life: When we are rebooting during a difficult time, we have to see it through to 100 percent completion. Otherwise, we have to start all over again.

Who wants that?

If you don't learn the lesson the first time, you get stuck with it again. So, take the hard way, learn the lesson, then move on to other opportunities.

CHAPTER 34:

Every Dreamer Needs a Cheerleader

The lovely young woman with flame-red hair and milky complexion peeping through a smattering of freckles cupped her chin in her hand and drummed the fingers of her other hand against the counter. She had been sitting there for two hours and had signed no more than five autographs, mostly for people who didn't know her but suspected she might be halfway famous and they had just missed hearing about it.

She wasn't. She had been hanging around Nashville for two or three years, trying to get something going, and though she had a record deal, nothing amounting to anything was happening for her. She couldn't break through. At Fan Fair that day, an event set up to bring fans together with country music stars, she was appearing in her record label booth, and I was directly across from her, manning the booth of the entertainment newspaper for which my sister was the editor. Since both of us had nothing to do, we struck up a conversation and passed the time as it idled by slowly. Later, from across the aisle I watched how bored she was and thought, "She should give it up and go home because if she hasn't made it yet, she's not going to."

She, though, was smarter than I. She didn't give up or crawl into discouragement. She hung in there. She didn't just wait for a better day to come. She, tough ranch girl that she was, took creative control of her music and began to turn out music that excited fans. A few years later, she won the coveted CMA Female Vocalist of the Year. Accepting the award, Reba McEntire held the statue up and, choking back tears, said, "This is for Mama." It was the first of hundreds of awards to come.

She dedicated the award to her mama because she had believed in and cheered her on when know-it-alls like me thought it was hopeless. Reba, truly one of the nicest people in show business, is the most accomplished star in country music having triumphed at everything she has tried from movies to television to Broadway to writing best-selling books. It started with her mama as her cheerleader, but for the last three decades, her husband, Narvel, has been her biggest encourager, always assuring her that no matter what, she could do it. Together as the dreamer and the cheerleader, they have become real doers and have proven that nothing can stop them. As a team, they are nothing short of amazing.

Every dreamer has to have a cheerleader or, as one of my friends likes to say, a "balcony person," the one who is sitting in the balcony screaming, "You can do it! C'mon! Keep going!" Throughout our lives, we will switch back and forth between dreamer and cheerleader. Sometimes we'll be the one chasing our heart's calling while other times we'll be the one who gives the extra push to the dreamer. If we can't encourage, we must, no matter how much self-restraint it takes, not be a discourager to another's hopes and dreams. Arguing against a person's dream will kill her soul.

As illustrated with Reba, I wasn't always that wise. Several years later, I proved I still had not learned my lesson. I dated, off and on, a racecar driver who had been very successful running a Midwestern short track series called ASA. Alan Kulwicki was a champion on that circuit and a superstar when he decided to step from a small pond into the big sea of NASCAR's top series. Suddenly he went from being a big fish making an astoundingly good living to being something of a nobody who was spending more money than he was earning.

I have never seen anyone face greater challenges than Alan. Nothing came easy. In fact, nothing came at all. Mostly it went. He was an independent car owner trying to compete against factory-backed teams with lucrative sponsorships. He had two racecars while other teams had a fleet of cars that designed specifically for road courses, superspeedways, or short tracks. When a wreck would demolish one of his cars, it would be an enormous setback while to another well-financed driver, it was a mere inconvenience. On top of this, Alan, serious-minded, brilliant, and quiet, was a Yankee in a land of Southern rednecks and good ol' boys. Most of the men he competed against had, at best, only high school degrees while Alan had a Masters degree in engineering. No one knew what to make of him, and he didn't know how to fit in. It was a classic example of a square peg trying to fit into a round hole.

One night over dinner in Michigan, Alan was particularly down. He was experiencing engine problems and, as a result, had barely squeaked into the field during qualifying.

"Everyone has a better engine program because they can afford it," he said. "Until I can make more horsepower, I can't compete. I'm just going to run in the back of the field, getting wrecked and tearing up my equipment." There were other challenges, too, and he talked about those. As he ticked off the problems he was facing, his face grew longer and his eyes clouded more. I knew how much money Alan had been earning on the ASA circuit and how much easier it had been. With that in mind, I offered my advice.

"Alan," I began sympathetically. "Why don't you just give up and go home? You're going to bankrupt yourself. If you go home, you can go back to making a good living and forget all these problems." I meant well. After all, it looked like a hopeless dream and that he was headed toward emotional and financial ruination. Alan was David in a field of Goliaths. He was out-moneyed, out-powered, and, as a result, outrun every week.

Discouragement of this kind works differently on different people. Some give in to it. Others are ignited by it. They are encouraged by the discouragement. That was Alan. He was slumped over the table but, suddenly, he drew back and squared his shoulders. He set his jaw and a new fire sparked in his dark brown eyes.

"No," he said firmly. "I will not give up. That is not an option."

Determinedly, he stayed the course. Times got almost downright desperate, but Alan, holding tightly on to his dream, refused to be deterred. After three years of almost insurmountable troubles, he won his first Cup race in a Ford Thunderbird that he, good-naturedly, had dubbed "The Under-Bird" for he was always the underdog. He kept building on that momentum and two years later, he claimed the series championship by a slim margin of ten points. Alan Kulwicki had come from nowhere, working with nothing, and beat the best drivers and heavily moneyed teams for the top prize.

Thank goodness he hadn't listened to me. I shudder to think how I boldly tried to kill a man's dream, and I ponder the sadness of it all if Alan had listened. I meant well. Most dream slayers do. I looked at the logic and financial risk and suggested that he retreat and save himself from going broke. It is embarrassing to remember that I tried to discourage someone so dear to me.

But I have learned this: dreams, especially the grand ones, make little sense to logical folks. Most dreams are liberal, not conservative, and they call for bravery and persistence. They demand that the dreamer stand strong and weather the adversity, knowing that after every storm, the sun reappears. A brighter day always dawns.

If you can't be a cheerleader then, by all means, do not be a dream slayer. You might discourage someone who is meant for great things like Alan was. And, also, there is no greater sin than that of robbing someone of hope. Learn from my grievous error: keep your mouth shut. It is fortunate that Alan had other cheerleaders around him and didn't have to rely on me for all his moral support.

Parents, well-meaning just as I was, sometimes make the same mistake when they see a child who has ambitions that seem off the beaten path. My friend Carolyn was not one of those parents. She raised two handsome sons, one who followed a traditional path into the corporate world while another was interested in the arts.

One summer I vacationed with Carolyn and the boys in Hawaii and while we were there, the youngest, sixteen at the time, made it clear: he was going to be an actor. While we lounged by the pool, his mother also made it clear: Whatever path he wanted to follow, she would support. She would not try to direct his life. As a result, Skeet Ulrich has found success as a movie and television actor. Both of her sons—Geoff who followed a white collar path and Skeet who followed an eclectic one—have made their dreams come true in different worlds. Their mother was always their biggest cheerleader. She still is.

Alan Kulwicki, the man who possessed the bravest heart of any dreamer I have known, was killed in a plane crash four months after winning the championship and reaching the sport's pinnacle. He was wearing the heavy gold championship ring. Though he was only thirty-eight years old, all of his dreams had come true.

The ending, of course, wasn't perfect, but the life story was beautifully written.

CHAPTER 35:

Love Someone Enough to Let Them Succeed by Failing

It's always our first urge to reach out and save those we love when they are in peril. When we have walked a similar path and gained wisdom from our own mistakes, we want to stop them from making the same mistakes.

Wisdom, though, is gained by experience, particularly when things go wrong. It is the consequences of mistakes that have the most resounding effect and give us a perspective that will cling like a spiderweb to the crevices of our minds. Though it's so difficult, sometimes we have to step back, sit on our hands, and not help our loved ones. Tough love comes when it hurts us to help someone in a way that seems counterintuitive—by not helping them.

There is a young woman who is so dear to me. For several years, going back to junior high, I have mentored her. She comes from a less-than-privileged background, but she has never whined about it or felt sorry for herself. She's remarkable in every way. She breezed through college by making the dean's list while working a part-time job, she volunteers in the community and church, is courteous and thoughtful, and manages her money superbly. She is a model citizen, as close to perfect as anyone can be. I am incredibly proud of her, so I have helped her whenever possible, especially in passing along lessons I have learned. Like a river thirsty for water, she drank it up.

Then came a time when she fell in love. Though beautiful inwardly and outwardly, she had never been particularly interested in dating. She was very sensible and concentrated on making a better life for herself. She was steady on the course. Oh, but the heart can take every lick of good sense away. We've all been there, right? The young man she began dating was pleasant, attractive, and cared for her. We liked him. But as time went on, it became apparent that he had suffered some emotional traumas that seriously impacted their relationship. He was possessive, demanding, and often argumentative. As time passed, the light faded from her eyes. Love became a heavy burden. When she talked about it and gave specific examples, I counseled her.

"The best a guy will ever treat you is *before* he marries you. He's on his best behavior now. If this is his best, you don't want to see his worst," I advised. Because she is so sensitive to the hearts of others, she did not want to hurt him.

"The longer you wait to break it off, the more it will hurt. You're pulling yourself down and leading him toward a greater heartbreak." Quietly, she nodded. Eventually, as I expected, she did the sensible thing—she broke it off. What a relief it was to see the light return to her eyes. Visibly, a load lifted from her shoulders.

Several months passed and I ran into a friend one day who mentioned the former couple. "What about them getting back together?" she asked. "I was so surprised."

I blinked, speechless. I talked to the young woman regularly. "Oh, you must be mistaken. They're not back together. She would have mentioned it."

Kathy shook her head and said slowly, "Noooo, I don't think I'm wrong. He told me the other day and showed me a coat that she had given him for his birthday two weeks ago."

My first instinct was that he had fabricated the reconciliation. I had known the young woman since childhood and had never seen her falter in judgment. Everyone has a downfall, though, regardless of how bright and intuitive they are.

I called immediately and asked. She stepped up to the plate and owned it. She admitted that she had decided to give him another chance. My heart fell because she's like a baby sister and I was and continue to be fully invested in her happiness. Of course, I wanted to argue against it and take full advantage of our friendship and mutual respect. Instead, I said, "Okay. You're a very smart young woman. You make good, solid decisions. I wish you the best."

"Is that all you're going to say?" my best friend asked when she heard how easily I let it go.

I nodded. "Yes, it is. In all the years I have known her, I have never seen her make a big mistake. It's remarkable for anyone, but especially a child who grew up with the disadvantages she had. If there was any way I could stop her, I would, but then she wouldn't learn. It's time for her to make a big mistake. None of us escape this life without making some doozies. She'll learn."

She did. And I was proud that I was able to overcome myself and my tendency to help someone so dear so she could learn a valuable lesson that she will never forget. It's awful hard to sway those who are in love, especially under the age of thirty. The heart rules the mind. It convinces us that people can change or that we can live with unpleasant behavior. The heart can see only as far as the next kiss while the mind can see much farther, if we allow it to show us. I was able to be a sage with my young friend because my parents were once that wise with me.

She eventually came back to me and said, "You were right. He finally showed his real self. I should have listened to you and spared myself so much heartbreak. It's been devastating."

"No," I replied. "You did exactly the right thing. You learned it for yourself. Otherwise, you would have never been satisfied or known if you made the right choice. Now, you know for certain."

I was in love with a handsome, good-hearted, funny guy. He had such a good personality and everyone enjoyed him so much. While there were wonderful things about him, there were some serious fundamental differences that kept us from being a good pair, especially a pair that could stay together for a lifetime. When we decided to marry, no one in my family, who could clearly see the differences, tried to dissuade me for they knew it would be impossible.

"Let her go," Daddy said to Mama. "She'll learn." Admittedly, it was easier for them than it might be for some people because they knew he was a nice guy, not one who would hurt me or cause irreparable damage. Whatever hurt I experienced could be overcome, while, at the same time, presenting a good life lesson. Five years later, just as expected, the marriage ended, and I walked away wealthy with knowledge. It informed future decisions and enabled me to make better choices. Armed with what I had learned from that marriage, I spent over fifteen years as a single woman, one who refused to settle for less than the ideal match. I was determined never to marry again unless I found a solid complement to my lifestyle and values. Two wonderful people do not always make a wonderful match.

Another time, Mama and Daddy bravely stepped back and let me earn my experience. I was twenty-four, just returned home from a stint as a sports writer at *USA Today* in Washington, DC. I was planning to return to *USA Today* when, out of the blue, a fantastic job offer came from a sports marketing firm in Indianapolis. Though I had never even seen Indy or been to the Midwest, I grabbed the offer. As youth is wrought to do, I put little thought into it because it was great money and working in a field I loved. I don't even recall thinking about it. I said, "Yes!" As soon as the agreement was made, I took myself to my parents' and made the big announcement, "I'm moving to Indianapolis." Most parents would have been a bit alarmed that their young daughter was moving eight hundred miles away by herself. They would have, at least, *questioned* it. Not my parents. They didn't bat an eye. They met my big announcement with the same reaction as if I had said, "I'm going to the grocery store."

They loved me enough to let me find my own success in life, even if it meant facing failures first. That's exactly what I did. I spent the next several years in a whirlwind of tries, failures, and an occasional success. In Indianapolis, I was miserably homesick. My next job was worst. But I learned. My failures, based solely on my own decisions, were the springboard to later successes. Big, out-of-the-box successes, which I would not have had without the benefit of those failures. Without mistakes, we have little wisdom and without wisdom, we'll continue to make poor decisions. Who wants to be forty or fifty years old and have no wisdom?

I have a friend who is always following behind her teenager, trying to spare him from the consequences of his choices. He's a great kid with a terrific heart and spirit but his judgment can be poor. "Leave him alone and let him learn from the consequences of his choices," I advised. "We all have to learn from our mistakes and we will make them because we can't escape it. You can't follow around after him for the rest of his life. Leave him alone and let him learn."

Mistakes and bad choices are part of every life. No one escapes, though the smart ones make fewer mistakes than others. For the most part, folks make smaller mistakes at seventeen than they make at thirty. And it's normally easier to recover from teenage mistakes than from adult mistakes because a teenager, due to lack of knowing better, is cut a wider swath of tolerance and forgiveness by others. Give your teenagers and young adults the best advice that you can give them, encourage them in the right direction but allow them to have some failures. The lessons they learn from those mistakes will help enormously in building a better tomorrow.

Remember: it's their lives and they have a right to earn wisdom through the lessons they learn. Then, one day, they can pester their own children and the others they love with their advice.

CHAPTER 36:

You Don't Always Have to Be the Best to Win

I t's too bad that sports are viewed primarily by men and for the reason of sheer entertainment when, in actuality, there are many lessons of encouragement and inspiration to be learned from team and individual competitions. Watching a sports channel on a regular basis is much more uplifting than the evening news and can certainly provide a textbook tutorial on overcoming adversity to find a better day.

As a sports reporter, I covered the ACC Men's Basketball Tournament one year and watched as a young freshman came off the bench to make an impressive jump shot. He was rather small but spunky. "What's his name?" I asked a sports writer beside me. We both picked up our roster sheets and checked.

"Michael Jordan," he said, shrugging.

"Never heard of him," I replied. As a sophomore, he had been cut from his high school team but after that appearance in the ACC tournament, he scored the game-winning shot against Georgetown in the NCAA championship game and the sports world sat up and took notice. When the high school coach tossed him aside, Jordan practiced harder and came back to tryouts the next year to earn a place on the team en route to becoming a legend. Who would have thought? That's the point, though—don't be concerned with what the world thinks your ability is or your chances of success are. Do not let someone else write on the slate of your self-esteem or dictate if you can succeed in whatever you take on. Believe in yourself and know that on any given day the circumstances can line up where you can emerge the winner, even if you aren't the best one in the game that day. You can't win if you don't play, but if you show up and play, you have a shot.

Over and over, I had an up close view to the ever present possibility of coming-from-behind to be the surprise victor. There is nothing more exhilarating and inspiring than to see the underdog become the top dog. It encourages all of us underdogs to believe in a better day when we, too, can out-better the best.

On that February day in 1990, the odds-makers were definitely giving long odds to Derrike Cope to win the Great American Race, the Daytona 500. To win, he'd have to beat star drivers like Richard Petty, Davey Allison, Darrell Waltrip, Bill Elliott, and the hands-down favorite, Dale Earnhardt, the toughest, most intimidating driver of all. Had you asked anyone in the garage that morning if Cope had a chance of winning, it would have been a resounding "Are you crazy? No way!" Anyone with such a ridiculous idea would have been laughed away.

After all, Cope had never won a NASCAR race, and he had been trying for over eight years. He had never even had a Top Five finish. A likeable, handsome guy, the truth is that he had never been a threat to win, so he wasn't taken seriously for any victory especially one in the pressure-filled, all-eyes-are-watching-on-national-television, most prestigious race of all. Earnhardt, on the other hand, was a threat every time he sat down in a racecar. He was fearless as well as feared. No driver in his right mind wanted to look in his rearview mirror and see Earnhardt tapping on his back bumper. By 1990, Earnhardt had already chalked up three championships (and would win it that year, too), as well as dozens of wins in the sport's top division. He, however, had never won the Daytona 500, the most coveted race of all. It is *the* race that every stock car driver dreams of winning. He was determined and when Earnhardt set his cap with determination, he was a force to be reckoned with.

The green flag fell, and Earnhardt proved he was serious about winning. He was pitch-perfect all day while few noticed that Cope was staying in the lead pack with good, quick pit stops and solid driving. With a few laps to go, the television guys noted that Cope was having a nice run, but acknowledged it would be hard to overcome the tenacious Earnhardt who was leading and determined not to be outrun. Still, no one took him seriously.

But sometimes fate has other ideas.

It was the last lap of the race, Earnhardt was headed toward the third turn, less than a mile away from grabbing the checkered flag he had been chasing for years when he ran over a piece of debris and shredded the right front tire. Expertly, he wrestled the car to keep from wrecking, slowing down and letting the car drift to the top of the embankment. We all gasped. No one could believe it. Earnhardt was within seconds of winning the one race he treasured most. My heart hurt for him, but on the other hand, it leaped with joy as Derrike calmly drove past him and, incredibly, claimed the victory. To this day, it is considered one of the greatest upsets—if not the greatest—in the history of the Daytona 500. Earnhardt managed to finish fifth. His team took the shredded tire, hung it up on the wall of the race shop, and used it as motivation to win that next year's championship.

Derrike, for his part, took his place in the history books as a Daytona 500 winner. He was never favored to win that race or any race, but he did what it takes to win—he kept showing up. He kept trying. He refused to let anyone destroy his dream or erode his self-esteem to the point where he thought he wasn't capable of competing with the best and beating them. In the end, he beat the toughest driver who had the best racecar. In a blink of an eye, things can change. Circumstances can turn around and the best in the game can be sidelined. Every morning brings an opportunity for you to have the best that day, to have a success that has long been your dream. It is a remarkable story that will, no doubt, be an inspiration to Derrike's children and grandchildren. They are certain to pass down the legacy of a man who kept trying until the trying paid off in a grand way.

One day Darrell Waltrip and I were discussing another unlikely winner of a recent race. He shrugged. "Well, the best car doesn't always win. I've lost races when I had the best car, but something happened. I've also won races when I didn't have the best car, but the best one fell out. It evens out, I guess."

A couple of years after that conversation, it was the Daytona 500 of 1989. Darrell, like Earnhardt (who did finally win the 500 in 1998), had been trying for seventeen years to win the prestigious race. "It means everything to me," he had said when we were in Daytona a month earlier to test for Chevrolet. "I've won dozens of races here at Daytona, but never the one that means the most. My career will never be complete if I don't win it."

Every year during the two-week period known as Speed Weeks in Daytona, there is always a clear favorite. The 500 kicks off the race season after a two-month layoff, so inevitably, some team really does its homework and shows up as the clear favorite. That year it was the immensely likeable Kenny Schrader who is funny, talented, and the most serious-minded driver you'll ever meet. He won the pole at a speed that was one and a half miles faster than the second place qualifier—Darrell Waltrip. Every race he competed in that week, he won. There was no doubt about it—Schrader was the driver with the car to beat.

On the day of the race, true to prediction, Schrader ran off and left the field. He was strong and confident. Waltrip, it appeared, was headed to his seventeenth disappointment in the Daytona 500. I was sitting with Darrell's wife, Stevie, in the pits as she scored the fuel calculation. When Darrell's crew chief asked her, with fifty laps to go, if it was possible to outlast the field on gas if there wasn't a caution flag stop for gas, she ran the numbers on her calculator. She shrugged. It would be an incredible stretch of seven laps. Later as I reflected on the conversations that took place before the decision was made—

Darrell expressed his opinion via radio—I realized that sometimes the big successes in life call for boldness. Big success, the kind that is remembered and admired, is not achieved by the faint of heart. It is accomplished by those who are brave and willing to fail big in order to win big. When the decision was made to try to stretch the gas, one thing was completely clear: Darrell Waltrip was either going to grab his dream in a glorious, stunning fashion or he was going to fail live on television in front of millions of people.

They chose to roll the dice, to step out of the box of comfort that would guarantee a Top Five finish and a lucrative pay day. They refused to settle. I marvel often at what a gutsy call that was because the payoff in the Daytona 500 is significant down through the finishes. A safe call would have given Darrell a Top Five finish and a much bigger share of the purse than fortieth place. Sometimes, though, you have to be willing to lose a lot in order to win a lot. The last five laps of that race were a series of emotional ups and downs, and twice Darrell was convinced he was out of gas. The CBS camera crew came to our pit to finish the anguish of those five laps, hoping to catch our tears and upset when Darrell ran out of gas.

At one point, a lap and a half away from the checkered flag, Darrell screamed into the radio that he was completely out of gas. Despair ran through our hearts. Stevie and I looked at each other with tears in our eyes and shook our heads. There are times when we can be close to holding our dreams in our hands, then it pulls away. It may even pull back to the point that we think it's gone for good. That's the time when we either let it go or chase it down. Almost without fail, our first instinct is to let it go. Though it appeared completely hopeless, Darrell began to maneuver the car, weaving from top to bottom of the highly banked track. He coasted into the next two turns before, when coming out of the fourth turn, the car found a swallow of gas that was tucked into the fuel cell somewhere. It was just enough to take him to victory while the best car of the day—the best by far—finished second.

Sometimes we win, even when it seems impossible, by being bold enough to take the chance. By swallowing down the fear that would paralyze us and stop us, we can succeed. If we give in and back out, we gain nothing and, possibly, we lose everything. I have often said that Darrell's 500 victory that day was the greatest lesson of my life because I, who was deeply emotionally invested in whether he won or lost, saw firsthand that you don't always have to be the best to win. The reality is that I have seldom been the best but I have won nonetheless when the circumstances lined up to put me in front of the best. Neither Darrell or Derrike Cope ever won another Daytona 500. That was their single victory in the sport's most prestigious race, but it only takes one to put a driver in the record books and give him the greatest accomplishment of his career.

They won because they didn't give up. They showed up, kept trying, and kept believing in the best to come. Don't be discouraged by the competition for a job, a promotion, or college admissions, just try your hardest and remember that on any given day, regardless of the long odds, you can come out the winner.

CHAPTER 37:

Every Life Teaches

There's no way that any of us could live long enough to learn all there is to gain from the experiences of life. And, quite honestly, we wouldn't want to go through many of the situations that others face in order to gain knowledge.

When I was seventeen, I became the youngest radio personality in the nation when a country music station hired me to host a weekend afternoon show. I threw myself into the job and began my reporting career in earnest by booking interviews with country music stars. I was diligent in research and preparing questions. This was in the pre-Internet era when it was much more difficult to find information, so my knowledge was impressive to the stars I interviewed.

One afternoon, superstar Ronnie Milsap, a fixture on both

pop and country charts, was hosting a press conference in his dressing room. Milsap, born blind, was abandoned by his mother at birth, raised until the age of five by grandparents who then sent him to a school for the blind. It was there that teachers realized that his gift for piano made him a child prodigy. His life, despite enormous success, had been filled with obstacles. That afternoon, there were several reporters there, and it soon became evident—I was the only one who had done my homework. I asked a question, and Milsap grinned, turned his face toward me, and said, "Tell me your name. You ask excellent questions."

The teenager in me giggled a bit, then I told him my name and the call letters of my radio station. He nodded. "When this press conference is over, please stay. I'll give you an exclusive interview."

People respond well to those who are genuinely interested in them and who ask thoughtful, probing questions. Once the others left, we settled on the worn, plaid sofa. I asked questions that I wouldn't have asked in front of others.

"If you could see, what would be the first thing you would want to see?" I asked.

He didn't think it was silly. "People. I'd want to see my wife and my son. Then I would want to see color. I'd want to know what red and blue are."

Simple things like that, we take for granted. Imagine if you had no comprehension of colors or trees or if you had never seen the faces of those you loved. He expounded a bit, giving me the courage to ask my next question.

"Does it make you sad that you've never had the opportunity to see things that you would want to see?"

His answer has stayed with me in the years since. "No." He

smiled knowingly. "You don't miss what you've never had. I never had my sight, so I haven't missed it. It's all I've ever known."

Milsap, in the short time I spent with him, was a teacher to me. He didn't have a strong start to life—it was marked with misfortunes—but he didn't use those early years as a crutch to keep from trying. He didn't lie down and give up. He accepted what it was for what it was and moved on with determination. Because he seized his musical genius, he moved forward to make his future the better days of his life. Some people allow an underprivileged childhood to define them, to dictate their future. They claim that they are unable to escape the setbacks of early years, yet Milsap, blind and abandoned by his mother, refused to allow his life to be crippled by what happened, what was completely out of his hands. Instead, he took control of the days ahead.

His philosophy was brilliantly simple—don't mourn the lack of eyesight or feel self-pity. He refused to miss what he had never known. Time wasted dwelling on setbacks will keep a life from being productive. Don't let a misfortune threaten future better days. Take it on the chin, pick yourself up and use it as a trampoline to bounce upward toward better times. Just like Ronnie Milsap did.

Corbin, Kentucky is like most rural towns that sprang up in the hollers of the Appalachian Mountains. It was built for practicality and function rather than for leisure and beauty. Like other towns built on the black dust of coal mining, it has a sadness about it for most people who are born there and die there—but it's the only life they can ever imagine knowing. It is a railroad town that borders the coal mines, which are both a blessing and a curse for they bring needed jobs, but coal mining, without question, is one of the hardest jobs in America. It is also one of the most dangerous, for it can kill a man suddenly with a mine collapse or a little bit at a time with black lung. Some, too, surely die from a broken heart, knowing that their children inherited from them a lifetime of barely getting by, for coal mining jobs are often passed from father to son.

I found Corbin and the man who became a hero accidentally. I was heading toward Lexington on I-75 when a friend called. Discovering that I was only a few miles from the Corbin exit, he said, "You have to stop in Corbin because it's the home of the first Kentucky Fried Chicken." Actually, it is the home of the Colonel Sanders Café, which is where he once had a gas station and café and where he developed the famous recipe. Loving history, I abruptly swung off the interstate and headed toward the landmark. When I walked in, I was greeted by a man with strawberry blond hair and a big smile.

"Okay," I began. "I'm Southern but I've never had a piece of fried chicken." His eyebrows shot up. I nodded. "I grew up on a farm, if you know what I mean." He got the point. If you watch a chicken prepared for the kitchen, it can definitely affect your eating habits. We discussed which I would choose (it's hard to beat the original recipe, he said), so he placed the order and we began to talk. His name was Junior.

"How long have you worked here?" I asked.

"Over twenty years." He grinned. "I'm the assistant manager."

My mouth dropped. "Twenty years? Here?"

He beamed. "Yes ma'am. It's a good job, and I'm proud to have it."

How extraordinary. Same job for over twenty years. In a fast food place. Assistant Manager. And he wasn't malcontented. He was as happy as he could be. He didn't spend his days wishing for better days. He took the precious days that came his way and embraced them for the best days they could be. He had the days that he wanted and ones that make him content. He wasn't working in a coal mine or doing hard labor on the railroad. He had a steady job with benefits, so he was pleased with his good fortune. A few years later, I excitedly suggested to my sister and niece that we stop at the café when we were heading down I-75.

"I want to see my friend, Junior," I announced. And sure enough when we walked in, it was Junior's smiling face that greeted us.

"Do you remember me?" I asked, grinning.

"I shore do. You had your first fried chicken here."

We talked like old friends and before we left, I asked Junior if we could have our photo together. One of my heroes he is. Since the day I met him, I have thought of Junior's enthusiasm and contentment. Sometimes better days are right in our grasp, but we don't see them because we want even better times. Junior, though, holds each day dear. He works hard, day in and day out. He is one of the cogs in the many wheels that keep America turning, yet few of us stop to think how important Junior and his kind are to all of us. Or that Junior, in his unique way, is as successful as Hollywood's biggest star. It's just that the world doesn't know his name.

On a later trip, Junior wasn't at the café because he has weekends off. As only small town folks would do, someone gave me his phone number, so I called him at home. He wasn't there, but his wife explained, "His mama and daddy aren't doin' well, so on his days off, he stays over there all day and night to take care of them."

My admiration grew by leaps and bounds. A good worker, a steady provider, and a dedicated son, a man who gives more than he takes from life and does it without complaint. He sees the good in every day and embraces it with a happiness that is contagious.

Few lives are easy, though some, admittedly, are easier than others. Like Junior and Ronnie Milsap, there are challenges, but there's always a way out, a path to a better day. More than likely, Junior will never have the wealth or fame of Milsap, but in his corner of the world, Junior is just as successful. I learned from both.

Every life—whether that of a common or a famous man— teaches. We have only to look. And listen.

CONCLUSION:

Your Better Day May Come Today

When I was newly graduated from college and living the typical paycheck-to-paycheck existence of a young career woman, I shared an ancient duplex with my best friend, Karen Peck. We were both following our dreams—mine as a writer and sports reporter and she as a singer and Christian entertainer.

Karen had boundless energy and unbridled optimism and was always looking for the best yet to come. Of course, as young twentysomethings, what we thought we wanted most was romance, so we spent a lot of time talking about the man of our dreams. Since we both traveled a lot, we often saw each other no more than two days a week. Still on those days, we would

crawl out from bed and gather, in our pajamas, over coffee in
the tiny living room. Most mornings, Karen would come
bounding down the stairs with a big smile and exclaim, "This
may be the day we meet our husbands!"

It became a joke to me, but Karen was dead serious. In her
eyes, every new day brought the possibility for one of her
dreams to come true. One day, we left our duplex in separate
cars, both heading off to our jobs. I stopped directly behind her
at a red light. As soon as her car stopped, she opened the door,
looked back at me, and yelled something. I didn't understand, so
I rolled down my window and leaned out.

"This might be the day!!!!!!" she was yelling. "We might
meet him today!"

I threw back my head and laughed, so young at the time
that I didn't see the wisdom in her words. You never know what
can happen in a day. Life doesn't spin around on our terms or
our schedule. How many times have you awakened in the
morning with your day scheduled according to your needs and
desires? But, lo and behold, when you went to bed that night
you had to admit that the day you had just lived was nothing
compared to your plans.

Today could be the very time that your better day arrives. It
could be minutes away from happening. It is inevitable that
better days return. Sometimes they arrive gradually, having
given you notice that they'll be landing soon. If your spouse is
stationed out of the country with the army, you probably know
when to expect him or her to return stateside. You have the joy
of anticipating that better day.

Sometimes, though, the sweetest better days arrive quickly
and unannounced.

Karen found her dream husband, married him, and had

two children. With that dream tucked away, she followed other ones. Precious joy is found in always setting goals and having dreams. To just go through each day mechanically is no fun and gives no fulfillment. As the years went by, she built her career stone by stone. She had number one records, won awards, and was nominated for Grammys. Many, many good things happened to her. Like everyone, she had periods when life was tougher than it was at other times. That's normal. But she always kept her optimism and when one goal was met, she set another.

At some point I talked her into going to an acting class with me. Besides being fun, I thought it would help us both in our careers—her onstage as an entertainer and I as a speaker. Within thirty minutes of being in the first class, Karen was completely bitten by the acting bug. As it turned out, she was quite good and immediately she became the teacher's pet who used Karen as the example for how to do things correctly. For a few years after that class, Karen carried in her heart the dream of acting in a movie or on a series. Always the optimist, she believed that anything was possible and that it could happen on any given day.

One day, she received a voice mail from a woman who said she was a casting director for a movie and wanted to talk to Karen about appearing in it. Karen was skeptical, even though the number came from a New York City exchange. She had done nothing to pursue any acting opportunities, other than daydream about them. Cautiously, she returned the call and what the casting director had to say simultaneously thrilled and dismayed her. She wasn't certain that it wasn't an elaborate hoax of some kind because it sounded too good to be true.

The casting director explained that the movie's director had asked her to call Karen and inquire if she would be in the movie. He had seen a clip of her performing online and thought she was perfect for the role he had. The movie, the woman explained, would be starring Queen Latifah, Dolly Parton, and Kris Kristofferson. What? It couldn't be.

She called me and as Karen tends to be when she's excited, she babbled at a hyper pace, talking so fast that I could hardly understand her. "I looked him up. The director. And he's legitimate. Can you believe this? Dolly Parton? Queen Latifah? Ohmygosh I can't believe this."

It was true, though. With one unexpected phone call, Karen, out of the blue, had a better day drop in her lap. It became the thrill of a lifetime when she acted in the movie—three lines—sang onscreen, got to enjoy the red carpet experience, and was featured in a bestselling sound track. Sometimes the best days don't announce themselves, they just happen when we least expect them. Karen had prepared herself with acting classes, so she was ready when the dream knocked on her door and presented itself.

A bit earlier, I was having some pretty good days. My career was going well enough to keep me busy and well fed and I was content personally. I had been divorced for fifteen years and never once had I lamented over whether I would find another husband or not. I was so grateful for what I had and my ability to make a living that my philosophy was, "If I meet someone, lovely. If I don't, I'm so blessed that I can't complain." So much goes into finding a perfect, lifetime mate because you have to complement and or understand each other intellectually, emotionally, spiritually, philosophically, culturally, passionately, and creatively. It's a bigger task than most people think. Still, I believed it was possible and it could happen. I just didn't bank on it. From time to time, I'd think of Karen and our early days and smile with the thought of, "It could happen today."

Karen was nominated for a Grammy for the second consecutive year, and I had promised that I would join her in Los Angeles for the festivities. Two weeks before the event, I had decided I needed to cancel because of some business obligations. I went to bed that night but couldn't sleep. My conscience kept me awake reminding me that I had given Karen my word, and I kept hearing Daddy say as he had always said when I was growing up, "When you give your word, you keep it. No matter what it takes. No matter what it cost you. Always keep your word." Finally, at midnight, I flung back the covers, turned on the light, picked up my laptop, and booked my flight.

What a remarkable choice that turned out to be. The second day I was there, I called into my office and had a voice mail from a man who said he was a television writer/producer in Los Angeles and he was writing a movie on Alan Kulwicki, whom I had dated casually, and he wondered if he might speak to me by phone. I arched an eyebrow. How amazing, I thought to myself. I'm here in Los Angeles right now. I returned the call and suggested we meet in person. Perhaps coincidences happen in the small things in life—like going to the grocery store specifically to buy coffee and discovering it's on a buy-one-get-one-free sale—but the big things aren't coincidence. They are things meant to be, but they seem like such an incredible coincidence that they really get our attention.

The producer, John Tinker, was equally astounded by the timing, underscored by the fact that it was the first time in two years that I had been in Los Angeles. Later, I would recall how I had tossed and turned that night when I was trying to find peace with my decision to skip the Grammys. That event brought to me a clear realization that often nudging—when we want to do one thing but our spirit pushes for something else—is an internal compass that is pushing us toward the right opportunity. When you feel a conflict, don't go with your wants, go where your compass directs.

The three-hour meeting seemed uneventful. We shook hands, he expressed kind compliments, I offered my help in any way, then good-byes were said, and we turned to walk off. Several feet away, a surge of knowing swept with a jolt across my body, my heart flipped, and suddenly, I realized that I had just met the man I was going to marry. I wasn't even looking. A trip across the country, the timing of a phone call, and the instilled principle of the importance of keeping my word had delivered me right into the hands of my future.

A better day had come when I wasn't expecting it, and it brought with it the promise of many additional better days to come. That morning when I had arose, had my coffee and dressed, I had no idea how abruptly my life was about to change. I did not have a clue that I was a few hours away from meeting the man who would become the most important person in my life. What a happy thought that is—that on any given day, when we least expect it, we can have a surprise that causes our hearts to explode with joy. Karen and I both received unexpected calls that led to unsurpassed joy.

Your better day may come today.

While life has offered me ample opportunities to learn from personal experiences as well as the experiences of others, there is much I still don't know. One of the biggest questions that haunts me is whether it is easier to lose a man to a pretty woman or an ugly one. I have lost both ways and found that my self-esteem took a hit each time. With the pretty woman, I felt blah and unattractive. With the ugly one, I decided that I must not look nearly as good as I thought. So, I'll file that question away and hope that I'm never put into either situation again.

I don't understand why pimentos are located on the vegetable aisle and not next to the stuffed olives where they obviously should be or why we put away special things, like a pretty nightgown, and "save it" for a special occasion, which never comes. It's beyond my comprehension why grocery stores offer antibacterial wipes to clean the handles of the carts or baskets but the drug store—where all the sick people go when they're at their sickest—doesn't. I don't know why some people choose to dive into self-pity over the smallest things while others who have every right to feel sorry for themselves rise up gloriously to inspire those around them. Like my friend Tammy, for instance, who lost her teenage daughter in a horrific car accident, then with amazing strength comforted those around her instead of the other way around.

I don't know why hard times come, why no matter how smart or prepared we strive to be, we still face tribulations. But I do know this—hard times pass and better days always return.

"This, too, shall pass," Mama used to say when trials came. "One day these hard times will be just a memory, if we even remember them at all." That's such a truth because many things that might be breaking your back today will probably be completely forgotten further down the road. Like childbirth. The memory of most difficulties fade away.

It was the day before Thanksgiving when I do a good deal of preparation and cooking for the next day's dinner. Debbie, one of my best friends for many years, had just endured a spirit-breaking week. It had been a thunderstorm of events, one after another. One bit of bad news would knock her to the ground, and just as she started to get up, she got hit again. It was a hodgepodge of everything bad you could imagine—financial, family, business.

"Why don't you come over and spend the afternoon with us?" I asked. "You and Tink can hang out while I cook. It'll do you good to get your mind off things." She agreed and it turned out to be just what the doctor ordered. We laughed, told stories on each other, and shared memories. When dinnertime came, I said, "Stay and have dinner with us."

As I was cleaning off the table later, I was struck by the pure joy on her face. That afternoon, I had seen her laugh like I had not seen in years. If we're not cautious, we can lose our laughter and that is one of the most serious losses in life. I watched one day as my niece's three-year-old twins began to giggle over nothing. Their giggling tripped into laughter, and then, suddenly, they were belly-laughing, bent over double from hysterics. Kids laugh like that because they have yet to know sorrow, hurt, or the setbacks of life. Their joyous laughter is derived from pure innocence. The challenge for all of us becomes to protect our sense of humor and laughter despite the hurts and sorrows we endure.

"I haven't seen you laugh like this in twenty years," I remarked quietly.

Still grinning and fiddling with the camera on her phone, she replied, "I can't remember the last time I did laugh like this." She shrugged. "It's been a long time." Suddenly, she thought of another funny story from our youth and began to tell it by saying, "Remember when . . ."

When that story finished, still smiling broadly, she sighed happily. "You know, you're right about better days do come again. The last three or four days? Not so good. But today? The most fun I've had in years. It was worth going through the last few tough days to get to a day as much fun as this one has been." When she left that night, armed with leftovers and homemade cookies, she was still smiling and laughing.

No matter how desperate life may seem now, things do turn around. John Kennedy Toole was a gifted novelist from New Orleans who, like many creative people, faced rejection of his work to the point that he was driven into depression and then to suicide. After he died, his book, *A Confederacy of Dunces*, was published, won the Pulitzer Prize for fiction, became a best seller, and he was touted as a literary genius. If he had just hung on, he would have seen the best of the better days. He took his life and missed them all. You may be in a period of life when it seems hopeless and filled with despair. Hang on. Better days are coming again. Or you may be content, in a place where you are not particularly overjoyed *or* unhappy. For you, an unexpected, happy surprise may be one phone call or e-mail away. You, too, have better days coming.

And that better day may come today.

Acknowledgments

This book, quite simply, would not exist without the steadfastness of my agent, Laurie Abkemeier. As times became more difficult for everyone, I longed to write a book filled with stories of people – both famous and not – who had crossed my path and inspired me. People who, when they hit a wall of adversity, could have given up but instead pushed through to find a better day.

Laurie, too, saw the good in this project and spent untold hours editing the proposal and pushing me to bring my best to the table. Her enthusiasm and diligence resulted in an auction among several publishers. I am so grateful to her for many things but, particularly, because she shared my vision and shepherded it into the very capable hands of editor, Jennifer Kasius.

Jennifer also saw the value in these stories from the moment her hands touched the proposal. An author cannot be more blessed than I to have such an enthusiastic agent and editor. My heartfelt thanks to both because we all know this: Someone will be touched by this book in a powerful way. Maybe there will be dozens or hundreds or more but the truth is: If our combined efforts help one person to find a better day, we have proven that the world of publishing is a public service as well as an art. Thank you, Laurie and Jennifer.

Darrell and Stevie Waltrip lend invaluable help whenever I'm working on a book by throwing open the doors of their secluded lake house and giving me free rein to live and work there as long as needed. Deep in the piney woods of Tennessee, I find the peace and quiet to write, unhindered by phones or normal distractions. God bless you my dear, precious friends. Your love and generosity is tucked into every word of this book.

My friends, Debbie Love and Karen Peck, and niece, Nicole, are a constant source of encouragement and thoughtfulness and are the best prayer warriors I could ask for. My deep, deep appreciation to y'all.

There are so many who touch my life and help me to do what I do every day: tell stories that entertain and inspire, whether it's in my newspaper column, speaking engagements or books. At the risk of unintentionally overlooking someone, I must thank all of my family and in-laws, wide circle of friends including Gregg Foxworthy, Richard Childress, Virgie and Bill Miller, Sandy Booth, Barclay Rushton, Sam Richwine, Rich Middlemas, Erin Still, Jane White and the many newspaper editors who entrust my stories to their readers each week. Thank you. And to Selena Nix, my niece, who did the photography and always does an amazingly good job, I appreciate you. Much gratitude is owed to many at Running Press from editorial to sales to publicity (Melissa Geller, Craig Herman) and marketing because they dove in, worked hard and delivered such a gorgeous looking book into the hands of booksellers and consumers. Thank you to all who touched this book in any way, most especially the booksellers who make everything possible in publishing.

Though this book is dedicated to my husband, John Tinker, I am indebted professionally as well as personally to him. His advice is always solid and his encouragement invaluable. Thank you, my dear Tink. I love you.

Because I believe in the power of prayer, I am grateful for the guidance of the good Lord as I am for the guidance and wisdom of Mama and Daddy, both who believed always in better days to come and have now found the best days of all.

Without question, it is because of the dedication of my fans and weekly readers who support my newspaper column, my newsletters, speaking engagements and other books that there is the opportunity to tell these stories. Without you, there might not be a market for another tome written by me. Your loyalty and support is paramount and I am so grateful.

To all who read this book, thank you. It is an honor and privilege to have you spend time within the pages of this book. I wish for all of you the best of the better days to come.